The Shaolin Butterfly Style

Nick + Cathy,

Thanks for all,

Mike

The Shaolin
Butterfly Style

Art of Transformation

Sifu Michael Fuchs, C.B.I.S.

Waterside Press

Printed in the United States of America

First Printing, 2019

ISBN-13: 978-1-939116-92-5 print edition
ISBN-13: 978-1-939116-93-2 ebook edition

Waterside Productions
2055 Oxford Ave
Cardiff, CA 92007
www.waterside.com

This book is dedicated to my martial arts teacher, Lao Shr Tao Chi Li (known in PaiLum circles as Pai Tao Chi), who taught us with great dedication and purity, always providing outstanding leadership. As he taught us, "love is our shield, knowledge is our sword."
And to his teacher, Dr. Daniel K. Pai, whose lineage this rare style comes from.
And to all true teachers of the arts everywhere and in all times, who have done so much good in the world.
The Path is the goal, generation to generation, may the blessings be.

Table of Contents

Foreword xi
Preface ·xiii

Chapter One: Butterfly Origins · · · · · · · · · · · · · · · · · · · 1
Shaolin · 2
Pai Lum · 11
Shaolin Five Form Fist · 23
The Butterfly's Mother · 27
Taiji/Internal Styles · 28
Southern Shaolin · 29
Northern Shaolin · 30
Ch'uan Fa (Quan Fa) · 31
Chinese Weapons Division · 31

Chapter Two: Kung Fu Essentials · · · · · · · · · · · · · · · 34
Kung Fu-ology · 34
Shapes and Forms · 36
Levels of "Xing" Training · 37
Internal – External · 39
Soft Styles · 42
External Styles · 43
Hard Styles · 44
High and Low · 46
Internal/External, High/Low · · · · · · · · · · · · · · · · · · · 48
Kung Fu Roots · 49
More Kung Fu Roots · 52
Zoned Out · 58

Chapter Three: Exploring the Butterfly · · · · · · · · · · · · 61

Butterfly Birth · 61

Butterfly Infinity · 63

The Butterflies Purpose · · · · · · · · · · · · · · · · · · 71

Butterfly as "Inner Connector Style" · · · · · · · · · · · · 73

Shaolin Five Form Fist "Xing" Outline · · · · · · · · · · · · 73

Butterfly Principles · 75

Chapter Four: Butterfly Foundational Methods · · · · · · · 80

Introduction · 80

General Curriculum · 81

Basic Training · 83

Break Stance and Ceremonial Bow · · · · · · · · · · · · · · 83

Stances, Stance Work, Breathing · · · · · · · · · · · · · · 87

Stretching Methods/Leg Exercises · · · · · · · · · · · · · 89

Strength/Power Building Methods · · · · · · · · · · · · · · 89

Other Stuff · 90

Conditioning /Tempering Methods · · · · · · · · · · · · · · 91

Qi Gong/Nei Gong · 93

Falling and Rolling Methods · · · · · · · · · · · · · · · · · 98

Blocking/Deflecting Methods · · · · · · · · · · · · · · · · 101

Apparatus/Training Equipment · · · · · · · · · · · · · · · 109

Striking Methods · 112

Multiple Techniques/Articulation Drills · · · · · · · · · · · 114

Sweeps, Takedowns, Throws · · · · · · · · · · · · · · · · 117

Application/Self Defense Sets · · · · · · · · · · · · · · · · 121

Forms Training · 125

Chin-na/Grappling Methods · · · · · · · · · · · · · · · · · 135

Chinese Weapons · 138

Sparring/free-fighting Training · · · · · · · · · · · · · · · 149

Living the Art · 152

Chapter Five: Shaolin Butterfly Curriculum · · · · · · · · · 157

General Description · 157

Progression of learning · 158

The 3 Seed Techniques and Drills ·160
Foundational Butterfly Methods ·171
Butterfly Applications ·190
Shaolin Butterfly Forms· ·214
Butterfly Techniques in Other Styles · · · · · · · · · · · · · · · · · ·219
Butterfly Transformations · 223

Caption and Credit Page · 225

Author's Biography · 227

Foreword

When I was contacted by my old friend, Master Michael Fuchs, to consider writing a foreword to his new book "The Shaolin Butterfly Style – Art of Transformation" I must admit I was less than enthused. My first thought was yet another "me too" how to – Kung Fu book.

Michael sent me the manuscript and I picked it up and read it straight through – very unlike me – to find a book on the arts that would engage my attention so resolutely. Of course one of the elements that bore great historical significance was the role played by the great Grandmaster Daniel Pai, a man larger than life with whom I had spent some time, during the formation of the Chinese Kuoshu Worldwide Promotion Association in the late 1970's. GM Danny Pai was quite legitimate – he was the "real thing" – and was so dynamic you would instantly sense his abilities by just being in his presence.

The book – "The Shaolin Butterfly Style – Art of Transformation" has been so well written by Michael that it becomes an instructional manual with the historical and philosophical significance required of a true transformation work. At the same time the book lays a framework for the physical development and technical description of both technique and application.

Whether you are a novice in the Martial Arts or one with decades of training you will most certainly gain knowledge and insight from experiencing – "The Shaolin Butterfly Style – Art of Transformation."

Most sincerely,
Grandmaster David M. Grago
Wing Pai Federation
www.wing-pai.com

Preface

Welcome to this introduction to the rare Shaolin Butterfly style of Chinese martial arts. My main motivation and purpose for writing this book is to share this virtually unknown style with the worldwide martial arts community, and thereby hopefully ensure that the art survives into the future. So many rare traditional arts have been lost and are being lost each day now, which is, as far as I am concerned, a needless shame. Each style that has been developed over the centuries and proven itself to be effective, unique, and valuable—such as this one—contributes to the intricate mosaic which makes up the grand cosmos of the world of martial arts, and thus should be preserved and even cherished as cultural legacies, the same as other arts and disciplines.

Martial arts are arts of living, not mere pugilism, and like all living things they must adapt to the times and places they find themselves in. In this case, this means that the custom of keeping the Shaolin Butterfly style as a "secret" style has outlived its traditional usefulness. It is time for her to fly free now and help to germinate and pollinate many other martial arts flowers. It is my honor to be able to assist in this process.

Being an introduction to this art, this book is *not* a thorough presentation of all of the possible applications and techniques of the style. I do provide examples of the key, core techniques and applications, however (the seed and root techniques). What this book *is* about is presenting a comprehensive overview of the art; its history and lineage, concepts and principles, purpose and applications, and place within the larger "Mother

System" she is the central component of. Additionally, this book describes the key foundational concepts and methods of this "Mother System" which serve as the foundation curriculum of the Shaolin Butterfly style, and in fact are elemental to many Chinese and Chinese influenced systems worldwide. People who train in any style of martial arts should find this book interesting and valuable, same for the general public interested in the arts. There is something for everyone here, novice to expert.

While I had an outline of this book percolating within for several years, it was my agent who provided the spark and inspiration to actually write it. Previously I had written a textbook on Reiki Healing Arts and had been trying to sell it on my own to publishers for several years- with no luck. Despite great reviews and praise for the book, including from the publisher of a leading book publishing company, I was having difficulty finding a home for that book (publishers prefer you have an agent). Well, after I was fortuitously introduced to my agent I asked that he help me get the reiki book published. Wisely, he suggested that we let that project rest for a bit as I had already sent it to many publishers, and he encouraged me to write this book on the rare Shaolin Butterfly style as a first step.

Writing the book was an interesting combination of ease and challenge. The easy part was as I am so familiar with the material once I had a good working outline writing the book was in fact a joy, not a chore. The challenging part was as I work full-time including over-time every week, there are only so many hours in a day. Most of the book was written on my day off, as well as during occasional downtime at work (luckily my work allows for this to be possible). I must admit that at times I was literally falling asleep, pen falling out of my hand, while I wrote and edited. At any rate, after a year of perseverance I was done. Typically I write very fast once I get going—my book on Reiki Healing Arts is a comprehensive textbook and was written in three and a half months—but I happened to be unemployed at the time so I had lots of time on my hands each day to write and edit.

So here we are, as I write this Preface the book is now in its final stage of preparation before being published, the cover is being made, and final editing and formatting are taking place. There are so many I need to thank for their invaluable assistance along the way. First and foremost great thanks to my agent and his editorial staff and everyone at Waterside Productions for their superb assistance, support, and inspiration. Thanks and appreciation to Master Glenn Newth for the connection and recommendation to him/them. Of course, I must especially thank my teacher, Lao Shr Tao Chi Li, for sharing this beautiful art with me/us, thus making this book possible, and to his teacher Dr. Daniel K. Pai and the lineage for preserving the art.

My heartfelt thanks and gratitude go to GM David Grago for writing the wonderful foreword to the book. GM Grago is a living part of the history of the arts in our nation and world and knew Dr. Pai, as well as being one of the highest rated and respected true lineage Grandmasters alive. Thus, it is quite an honor for him to do this and so appreciated.

Special thanks as well to GM Clarence Cooper for allowing me to interview him regarding his experiences learning and making use of the Shaolin Butterfly style. GM Cooper learned the style directly from Dr. Pai going way back to the early 1970's and is regarded as one of the very top full-contact fighters of his era (Dr. Muang Gyi told me he was the best worldwide for a time). He made great use of the Butterfly methods in many full-contact bouts. Sharing his insights into learning, training and putting the style into practical effect with me is so appreciated and an invaluable contribution to this book.

Thanks to my photog, Stephanie "The High Vibe Chick" Stanton, and to those who appeared in some of the photos with me, or assisted in posing for photos: Sifu Michael Bogatay (Dao Li Shen), Master Giancarlo Fusco, and Sifu Donald Kinnie- Salutes!!

L-R, Master Giancarlo Fusco, Sifu Dao Li Shen, myself,
Sifu Donald Kinnie

Finally, I need to thank those who provided invaluable typing and editorial assistance, especially Ms. Christina DiTomasso and Ms. Devin O'Doherty- great job!

And to my parents and the Universal Life Force, for without their love and nourishment I would not be here- Namaste.

Sifu Michael S. Fuchs
1/4/2019
West Hartford, CT

Chapter One: Butterfly Origins

Butterfly Lineage

It is my distinct honor to be able to present this art and material to you. To the best of my knowledge the very rare "Butterfly Style" of martial arts has never before been seen in print. In fact, Butterfly Styles are so rare that they are virtually unknown.

My teacher, White Lotus Shaolin Five Form Fist Headmaster, Tao Chi Li, began training in Asian martial arts in 1961. He was born in Okinawa shortly after the end of WWII. Due to his many talents and intense discipline, he became one of the leading pioneers of the arts here in the United States. From the 1960's through the 1990's he learned from many of the top world level teachers of diverse martial arts, traveling all over North America, Hawaii, Taiwan, Hong Kong, Okinawa, and Japan. In all that time and through all those travels he told me that he only met two martial art teachers who had preserved and taught distinct "Butterfly Styles" (rather than say, concepts or a few techniques only). The material in this book comes from one of them, his main teacher the famous Grandmaster, Dr. Daniel K. Pai. Specifically, it is known as the "Shaolin Butterfly Style," and is a High, Internal Shaolin Kung Fu style. Just what those words mean and symbolize we shall be discussing throughout this book.

In this first chapter we are going to explore the lineage of the "Shaolin Butterfly Style," so that people understand that what I am presenting comes from a true source and transmission.

The place to begin that is to talk about something with a legendary mystique – Shaolin.

Shaolin

First of all, I am relying on sources which have direct connection to pre-Revolution Shaolin lineages and knowledge (as in the Chinese Revolution of the last century, which was won by the forces of Chairman Mao Zedong, founder of the P.R.C.). There is an old saying, "the history books are written by the victors." These history books may or may not be accurate, so a good researcher will consider as many sources as possible. In the case of Asian martial arts, much knowledge is preserved and passed down through reliable lineages which exist distinct from the vagaries of politics.

These sources include my teacher, who is the Headmaster of an actual Shaolin lineage. His teacher was the Shaolin Grandmaster Wu Jen Dai, who immigrated to Taiwan from the mainland around the time of the Revolution; which is where he met him in the mid-1970's while there with Dr. Pai and the White Dragon Society.

Another source is the writings of the famous Shaolin Grandmaster Wong Kiew Kit of Malaysia, who is the head of a true Shaolin lineage which was untouched by the politics of the Revolution. He is also a Buddhist Teacher in the Shaolin Chan tradition, and has Taoist Taiji lineage. I consider him to be one of the world's leading experts on traditional Chinese martial arts and their philosophies and training methods. An additional source of information is the website www.shaolin.com which also comes from traditional, pre-Revolution Shaolin sources and lineage.

I do not want to stray very far into politics, but it is important to understand that what is being disseminated by the modern, P.R.C. state-sponsored Shaolin Temple is a distinct re-interpretation and branding of the traditional arts and wisdom. To quote the current Abbot of Shaolin, Shi Yongzin,

"If China can import Disney resorts, why can't other countries import the Shaolin Monastery?" (Xinhua, March, 2015). Shi Yongzin has been called Shaolin's, "C.E.O. Monk." Now, comparing Shaolin – China's "foremost temple under Heaven" – to Disney is akin to equating the Vatican with Las Vegas. Beyond the crass commercialism of it, it is preposterous and degrading. Having said that, we will now move on from modern, sport wushu Shaolin and the Shaolin Commercial Empire – to the traditional version. Fare thee well all those who seek the Shaolin Path – let the buyer beware.

The Shaolin Monastery

The Shaolin Monastery was founded in 495 C.E. by the Indian Buddhist Monk Batuo (his Chinese name), at the behest and under the patronage of the Emperor of the Northern Wei Dynasty, Xiao Wen Di. Thus, right from the beginning Shaolin was an "Imperial Temple," very important in bringing Buddhism to China and disseminating it all over the Empires/Nations of China and surrounding regions throughout history.

The Temple was built at the base of the Great Central Mountain, Shao Shi, one of the 5 Sacred Chinese mountains. The mountain and surrounding lands were covered with pine forests, thus leading the Temple to being referred to as the "Shao Lin Temple" or "The Young Pine Forest Temple." To this day the evergreen pine is one of the symbols of Shaolin. In modern times the Shaolin Monastery exists in Dengfeng County, Henan Province, China.

The early, earth – shaking, watershed moment at Shaolin happened when the 28th Buddhist Patriarch, Bodhidharma, arrived there and began teaching, around 527 c.e. Some years earlier he had been invited to China to teach Buddhism by Emperor Liang Wu Di of the Northern Wei Dynasty. Bodhidharma, or Damo as he is known in Chinese, was the son of a King of a wealthy Indian kingdom. Like Lord Buddha himself, at a certain point he renounced royal life; eventually rising to become the 28th Patriarch in a direct line of succession from the "Awakened One."

Emperor Liang Wu Di was a Buddhist, still novel at the time in China, and had been very busy building temples, having scriptures translated, and performing other good works. Arriving at the Royal Court, Bodhidharma immediately began teaching, attempting to dispel some of the Emperor's illusions and giving him some "Buddhist Straight Talk." As described succinctly by Grandmaster Wong Kiew Kit, he attempted to teach the Emperor the first lesson of Buddhism which is "emptiness, not holiness."[1] This mirrors my own experience learning from my Buddhist teacher (of a different Mahayana Sect than Shaolin Chan). Our very first meditation was to "meditate upon the emptiness within emptiness."

The Emperor had been looking for validation of his good works in promoting Buddhism in China. Like all true spiritual teachers Bodhidharma only sought to lead him to Self-Realization, his "Buddha Nature." It reminds me of a story I read about a Buddhist Temple here in the U.S. headed up by a senior Tibetan Lama. His students had arranged for several wealthy potential donors to visit. When it came time for them to meet the Lama, he began by telling them that "they were all going to die" and shared basic Buddhist teachings on karma with them. Needless to say, they received no donations that day.

At any rate, Emperor Liang's ego was not happy with Bodhidharma's teachings and he was dismissed from the Royal Court. For a wonderful description of the famous meeting of Bodhidharma and Emperor Liang see *Kung Fu: History, Philosophy, Technique* by Chow/Spangler.

Bodhidharma thereby traveled to the Shaolin Monastery, and after some more trials and tribulations was invited in and assumed leadership of the Temple.

---

1 Wong Kiew Kit, The Art of Shaolin Kung Fu (Element Books,) 186.

Shaolin Kung Fu

Being a Royal Indian Prince of his time and place, from childhood Bodhidharma would have received the best instruction available in a wide range of arts, sciences, philosophies, and disciplines. This would have included yogic arts, including no doubts, both armed and unarmed fighting arts. Attaining the status of 28th Patriarch of Buddhism meant he would have had unparalleled knowledge of Buddhist meditative and yogic methods, as well as Buddhist and Indian philosophical knowledge.

Upon assuming leadership at the Shaolin Temple Bodhidharma found the monk's there to be in terrible physical and mental condition, due to their ascetic lifestyle and conditions. They were so weak that they couldn't practice any of the meditation methods which he attempted to impart. Buddhism being known as the "Middle Way" he then began teaching them the importance of a strong mind in a strong body. This included teaching them special methods for circulating qi and building vitality from the inside out, based upon his great knowledge of and experience with Buddhist and Indian yogic arts. The methods Bodhidharma taught these monks became known over time as the "18 Lohan Hands" and "Muscle/Sinew Metamorphosis." These methods proceed from the external to the purely internal: postures → muscles → sinews/tendons/connective tissues → marrow/brain/spaces. They constituted a complete system of outer/inner yoga, the goal being the health and vitality not only for long life, but to attain Self-Realization ("Returning to Original Nature").

Being the foremost Imperial Temple over the ages many important, educated, and accomplished individuals have visited Shaolin and trained, taught, and retired there. This includes military officers and others with martial arts training and knowledge (martial arts training has existed since pre-historic times in China, long before Shaolin existed). Over time the yogic, meditative, and spiritual teachings of Bodhidharma and Shaolin became fused with the native Chinese martial arts knowledge; as well as with Taoism and Confucianism. This blend of knowledge and martial arts training became systematized and taught as one of the jewels of Shaolin knowledge; along with Shaolin Qi Gong and Shaolin Chan (Zen), the pinnacle of the Shaolin teachings.

The idea of Buddhist monks practicing Kung Fu is not as strange as it might sound. The monks, disciples, and students of Shaolin had a right and a need to protect themselves, the same as anyone else; and developed highly sophisticated and effective ways of doing so. Ideally without violence, but if violence was offered to them and it couldn't be avoided, they would seek to redirect it. Barring this, the "offering" of violence would be returned to the "giver" as an unwanted gift, in as least damaging a way as possible. This is exactly how I was taught kung fu and taiji, by the way. The first level being to "redirect negative energy of word, thought, or deed" and the higher level being to "act previous" – avoid or neutralize negativity (including physical violence) before it manifests.

So, this systemization of the teaching of kung fu over the centuries led to our current understanding and the flowering of Shaolin Kung Fu influenced martial arts world-wide. "Indeed, Kung Fu, as we understand it today, started from Shaolin."2

Of course, Shaolin disciples and students, including Master Teachers, would leave the Temple and enter or re-enter secular life occasionally; further spreading the Shaolin arts, including kung fu arts. Chinese culture and civilization being ancient and spread out all over planet earth, the original Chinese Shaolin arts have been extremely influential in the development of the martial arts world-wide. As the old saying puts it, "all martial arts under heaven arise from Shaolin." And one of these Shaolin influenced and lineaged arts is the subject of this book, the Shaolin Butterfly Style.

Shaolin Chan

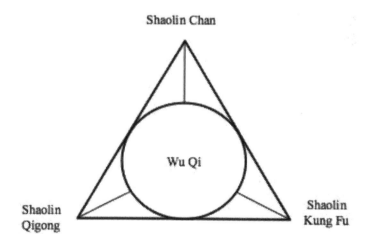

<hr>

2 Wong, The Art of Shaolin Kung Fu, 13.

The Three Treasures of Shaolin

As this is a book on a rare Shaolin Kung Fu Style, Shaolin Qi Gong and Shaolin Chan (Zen) are not the main focus. We will discuss Qi Gong a bit in a later chapter; but as it is the consummate gift of Bodhidharma and Shaolin, the highest attainment, I would like to at least introduce Shaolin Chan here.

"Shaolin Chan" refers to a then novel type of Buddhism which was emphasized at the Shaolin Temple, and has been very influential since as a major sect of the Mahayana Buddhist school. It is the Buddhism which Bodhidharma taught. The Chinese term "Chan" is better known as the Japanese "Zen" and the original Indian "Dhyana." They all refer to a state of profound meditative union or absorption, one where the separation of self and other—meditator and subject of meditation—have fallen away.

Classically, in the teachings of the "God of Yoga," Sage Patanjali (pre-Buddhism), Dhyana is known as the "7th Limb of Yoga." The "8 Limbs of Yoga" being:

1. Yama's – The Don'ts of Yoga
2. Niyamas – The Do's of Yoga
3. Asana – Postures
4. Pranayama – Breathing Exercises/Qi Gong
5. Pratyahara – Sense Withdrawal
6. Dharana – Concentration
7. Dhyana – Meditation
8. Samadhi – Enlightenment

Buddhism, of course, arose in India and sprang forth as an anti-dote to the problems Lord Buddha as the "Spiritual Doctor" identified in the culture and spiritual/religious teachings of his time. Dhyana as a practice in the various Buddhist schools and sects is understood differently, with some emphasizing it (such as Shaolin Chan); and others not so much (such as in Tibetan Buddhist sects).

Essentially, there are two broad main categories of Buddhist meditation: Shamatha and Vipassana. Shamatha meditation is referred to as "one pointed" or "tranquility meditation," and emphasizes Chan/Zen/Dhyana. Oftentimes the breath is used here as the subject of meditation, so that distraction and duality may be transcended and tranquility and higher states of consciousness achieved.

Vipassana Meditation refers to "insight" or "wisdom" style of meditation; Vipassana is sometimes also referred to as "contemplation." One enters a meditative state, then contemplates a question, topic, concept, or subject; the goal being to achieve deeper insight and wisdom, and ultimately, enlightenment (Kensho, Satori, or "Returning to Original Nature"). A typical Vipassana Meditation being to meditate upon the question, "what is the original nature of the mind?"

It must be emphasized that Lord Buddha taught and expounded upon both styles of Buddhist meditation. In the Tibetan Buddhist tradition which I took refuge in (Refuge is like Baptism, how one becomes a Buddhist) we learned about and practiced both; though the Vipassana style was emphasized. My Shaolin Kung Fu teacher also taught both, referring to them as "meditation" and "contemplation." In his teaching he viewed "contemplation" as the higher style; though we learned many versions of Shamatha Meditation, as well.

In fact, all of Shaolin Kung Fu practice may be thought of as a kind of Shamatha Meditation, beginning with the Kung Fu Salutation – the seed of the entire art of Shaolin Kung-Fu – and the Horse stance. Shaolin Chan and Shaolin Kung Fu are completely inter-mixed. Keep in mind, one need not be Buddhist to be Shaolin. Shaolin teachings are extremely flexible and have been practiced by people of all faiths – or none – for centuries. For instance, the Buddhist ideal of "Self-Realization" is in fact "No Self" – Lord Buddha having taught "anatman," or no soul. Buddhist Enlightenment is variously referred to as "Returning to the Original Nature," Busho, Kensho, or attaining Satori. It has to do with transcending all duality. It reminds me of the joke of the Dalai Lama and the NYC hot dog vendor. When asked what kind of hot dog he wanted, the Dalai Lama replied, "make me one with everything."

Well, a Christian or Muslim or Jew might think of this as being "one with God" or the like.

Grandmaster Wong Kiew Kit has written extensively on Shaolin Chan/Zen, including devoting an entire book to the subject, *The Complete Book of Zen* (Wong, Element Books, 1998).

I must again thank my teacher, as all of the major forms of Shaolin Chan/Zen which Grandmaster Wong describes were taught to us. This includes the Anapanasati Meditation of Tathagata Zen (ru lai chan); cao dong chan (Soto Zen, or, "no-mind" Zen); lin ji chan (Rinzai Zen, emphasizing use of koan's); and the highest method of the Shaolin Tradition (a method of Patriarch Chan, focusing on the void/emptiness), described by Grandmaster Wong as to, "go into deep meditation in a lotus position and keep your mind free of all thoughts." My teacher had a special way of leading us into this, which included chanting an ancient sacred mantra, and then the meditation on the "void."

A few final words on Shaolin and Shaolin Chan before we move on. The essence of Buddhism, and thus Shaolin, may be boiled down to these words of the Buddha himself:

"Avoid all evil,

Do good,

Purify the mind."

The Five Basic Buddhist Precepts are the following:

- No Killing
- No Stealing

- No Lying
- No Sexual Misconduct (sex with children or animals)
- No intoxication

These "don'ts" are very important to establish a foundation for doing good, which is emphasized by the 6 Paramitas (Virtues) of Mahayana Buddhism (including Shaolin Chan):

- Generosity/Charity
- Virtue/Morality
- Patience/Tolerance
- Perseverance/Effort
- Meditation
- Wisdom

It is from this noble and rich tradition that the Shaolin Butterfly style of Kung Fu was born. Let's explore now it's roots in modern times, how and by whom it was preserved and passed on, which has made this book possible.

Pai Lum

Now that we have explored Shaolin, the birthplace of the Shaolin Butterfly Kung Fu style, let's look at how it was preserved and passed on in modern times. In Chapter 3 I share the origin story for this rare style. How I came to learn what I did of it came through my teacher, and his teacher, the famous Grandmaster, Dr. Daniel K. Pai.

160 THE HARTFORD COURANT: Sunday, October 8, 1972

Pai and Ali

Dr. Daniel Pai of Hartford and Muhammad Ali pose for a picture at a recent Karate tournament in Pennsylvania near Ali's training camp. Pai, a high-ranking black belt in several forms of the martial arts, has been advising Ali and acting as his "bodyguard" before fights (Cruickshank Photo).

Ali's Body Guard
Gentle But Thorough

By KEN CRUICKSHANK

When Muhammed Ali walked the ring for his recent bout ith Floyd Patterson, he was ccompanied by a "bodyguard" om Hartford.

Not that Ali needs any help to efend himself, as he proved at night in the ring, but before bout he is often mobbed by admirers, jostled by hecklers or owded by curious onookers. Before the Patterson fight a an simply grabed his hand

Dr. Pai believes that some of Karate can be applied to boxing. Many of the techniques would be illegal, of course—especially kicking—but Pai says the "Chi" will be especially helpful.

"Chi" is the inner strength that is developed through meditation, concentration and practice.

"Every good athlete has Chi in some measure," Pai said in an interview recently. "He must

The Hartford Courant, 10/8/1972

12

Dr. Daniel K. Pai, photo courtesy of Christopher Lee Helton

Dr. Pai was one of the giants of the arts in the 20th century, a national and international pioneer and leader. It has been some time now since he passed on (5/28/1993), and most of his students keep a low profile, so apparently he is now a, "forgotten giant." In their end of the century edition the now defunct but once great magazine, "Inside Kung Fu," compiled a list of the, "100 Most Influential Martial Artists of the 20th Century." Dr. Pai was on this list, described as an, "American Kung Fu Legend," and an "early, driving force," of the arts. Although not a tall man, he cast a huge shadow, influencing so many. Every person I have met who knew him or even just met him once, described him as an unforgettable person. A true Hawaiian Kahuna of the arts.

Dr. Daniel K. Pai, Dragon Wing Ice Break, from CT Magazine, 1973, photo by Mr. David J. Everett

Dr. Pai was one of the National Chief Instructors of the United States Karate Association, founded by G.M. Robert Trias in 1948. The U.S.K.A. was the first national martial arts organization in the USA. Dr. Pai became a living legend in his own time due to his constant promotion of the arts, thorough mastery of the arts, and his famous demonstrations of seemingly superhuman feats.

United States Karate Association Chief Instructor, Dr. Daniel K. Pai, standing 2nd from right; USKA Founder, GM Robert Trias, kneeling in center; USKA Chief Instructor, Dr. Maung Gyi, kneeling 2nd from right; Bill "Superfoot" Wallace, standing far left; GM Jim Cravens, standing 3rd from right; various other Masters and champions of the USKA

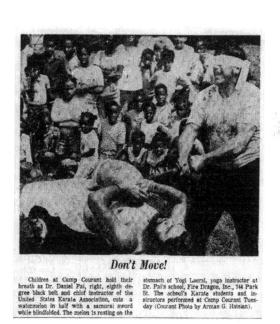

Don't Move!

Children at Camp Courant hold their breath as Dr. Daniel Pai, right, eighth degree black belt and chief instructor of the United States Karate Association, cuts a watermelon in half with a samurai sword while blindfolded. The melon is resting on the stomach of Yogi Laeral, yoga instructor at Dr. Pai's school, Fire Dragon, Inc., 744 Park St. The school's Karate students and instructors performed at Camp Courant Tuesday (Courant Photo by Arman G. Hatsian).

Dr. Daniel K. Pai blindfolded and slicing a watermelon to pieces on the abdomen of his student, Yogi Israel Segarra, Hartford Courant early 1970's

My teacher learned this material from him (the Shaolin Butterfly Style) in the 1970's. He began his martial arts odyssey in 1961 after being born on Okinawa shortly after the end of WWII; and earned multiple, old-school black belts from top teachers of the time. Legends such as Mas Oyama, Koichi Tohei, Robert Trias, Ken Ota, Shigeru Oyama, Tadashi Nakamura, and others. After living, training, and going to school in California for a few years, he returned to the East Coast. On a visit to the local YMCA to visit one of his old Karate teachers by "chance," he ran into the great master, Dr. Daniel K. Pai, who was teaching a class there (1972). It was a fortuitous meeting to say the least. Within 6 months my teacher had earned the distinction of being Dr. Pai's "Chief Instructor" at his Headquarters school in Hartford. And within 6 more months he was named "Chief Instructor" of the entire Pai Lum system. He also had the honor of being Dr. Pai's live-in student/disciple for a few years and was trained to be his successor. He served as "Chief Instructor" of the Pai Lum system until about August 1980 when he separated from Dr. Pai's organization for personal reasons.

My teacher, Lao Shr Tao Chi Li, double butterfly knives, 1980

Thus, he learned Dr. Pai's arts directly from the source; and since he was being trained to be a successor, in infinite detail. My teacher is a martial arts prodigy, blessed with iron discipline and a virtual "total recall memory" for the arts. For instance, he can still perform and knows the Japanese names of the Judo techniques he began learning in 1961. He will face us as we perform a form (Kuen/Kata) and perform it left-handed; then turn around and perform it right handed. Suffice to say the material he learned from Dr. Pai was transmitted purely and accurately to us (one of his duties as "Chief Instructor" was Quality Control of the Pai Lum system).

My teacher, Lao Shr Tao Chi Li, 1986

I myself began learning this material around 1992 with a small group in closed door "Sifu/ Disciple" classes. Our teacher felt the Shaolin Butterfly Style material was so special and key to our art and system that he directed us to not only not show it to anyone, but to not even talk about it! This included even lower level instructors. Later on he opened up a bit and even taught some public seminars on the art, opening the door for a book such as this.

Sifu Michael Fuchs, brand new Assistant Instructor/ Shr Shyung, 1990

I trained with my teacher for 17 years straight full-time, no breaks; including taking over the school from him and serving as "Chief Instructor" of the school and system for seven years. I always enjoyed and appreciated the Shaolin Butterfly Style and have continued practicing it, for over 25 years now. I now know from my own experience why my instructor felt it was so special, which we will be discussing and illustrating in subsequent chapters.

Now, I notice there is much confusion out there regarding Dr. Pai and his arts. For instance, in 2016 I attended a large martial arts expo (Expo 10 in Atlantic City, put on by Sifu Cliff Kupper), there were over 100 demonstrations featured by experts from numerous styles. I mentioned to an elder Hung Gar (a Chinese Style) teacher that I was going to be demonstrating Taiji Sword and Saber from Dr. Pai's tradition and a puzzled look came over his face. He responded, "but Dr. Pai was Hawaiian, he didn't teach Chinese martial arts." Shortly after I went out and did my demonstrations of obviously Chinese style Taiji and he just scratched his head. I have read and been told similar many times.

"Pai Lum" was the system which Dr. Pai developed based upon his life-time (never ending) study of Asian martial arts. The best translation I have seen is "Pai's Martial Forest" courtesy of Sifu William Luciano. Dr. Pai, you see, was born an illegitimate bi-racial child in Hawaii (4/4/1930). He was adopted by his "Grandfather", a lineage-holding Chinese martial arts grandmaster who had immigrated to Hawaii from the Singapore region (see the article, "The Incredible Feats of Dan Pai: A Master of Kung Fu," from "Connecticut Magazine," 1973).

Dr. Daniel K. Pai, Bruce Lee, Grandmaster Jhoon Rhee, Grandmaster George Dillman, L-R, early 1960's, courtesy of Mr. George Dillman

As a young boy he began training very intensely under his Grandfather on the pristine beaches, mountains, forests, and fields of Hawaii in the 1930's. He learned various pure Chinese styles from his Grandfather, including Pai Te Lung Quan Fa (White Dragon Kung Fu), Pai Yueng and Wu Chun Taiji, the Shaolin Butterfly Style, and others. So he was indeed a life-long practitioner and teacher of Chinese martial arts, and inherited his Grandfather's lineage as the succeeding Grandmaster. However, being a Hawaiian/American growing up in Hawaii at this seminal time in martial arts world history, he was very smart and began learning from many of the top teachers who resided in Hawaii. This included top teachers of all styles, but especially Hawaiian, Chinese, Okinawan, and Japanese styles.

Thus the "Pai Lum System" is an amalgamation of all of his vast martial arts knowledge. He also had a habit, like many great teachers do, of tailoring his art to each student. Apparently, no two Pai Lum teachers were taught the same thing or learned the same curriculum. Thus the confusion over just what the "Pai

Lum System" is or isn't. Some of the teachers and lineages tend to lean towards the Okinawan/Japanese side of the spectrum; others are more obviously Chinese style. Regardless, everything Dr. Pai taught was of high quality. No less an authority than famous living legend Grandmaster, Dr. Maung Gyi told me at a clinic he was teaching when I first met him in the Spring, 2001, "THE PAI LUM SYSTEM IS ONE OF THE GREATEST SYSTEMS IN EXISTENCE – FEARED EVEN IN CHINA!"

Sifu Michael Fuchs with Dr. Maung Gyi, circa 2004

I put this in caps as Dr. Gyi was shouting the words to me, so excited he was recalling his old peer and friend, Dr. Daniel

K. Pai. Very high praise as Dr. Gyi is regarded by many to be the world's greatest living expert and authority on the Asian martial arts.

Back to the Shaolin Butterfly Style. While the " Pai Lum System" is indeed a synthesized system, it is also quite traditional: within it are preserved numerous traditional training methods, philosophies, and styles – the Shaolin Butterfly Style being one of them. Preserved and passed down from Dr. Pai's Grandfather to himself; then to my teacher; and then to me. Nothing has been changed. Now you can learn about it as well.

Shaolin Five Form Fist

As mentioned, my teacher left Dr. Pai and his organization late in 1980. However, he was far from being done with training and teaching. This section is integral to the story of how the Shaolin Butterfly Style was preserved and passed on from Dr. Pai's Grandfather, to Dr. Pai, to my teacher, and then to me. It also describes the Shaolin Butterfly Style's place and importance within my teacher's overall system, the Shaolin Five Form Fist System (Wu Xing Quan Fa).

Amongst his many accomplishments, Dr. Pai is the pioneer and Founder of the Koushu movement and arts here in the United States. The Koushu (Guoshu) Movement began in mainland China, before the Revolution. The government at that time in China wanted to preserve and pass on their great cultural legacy of the Chinese martial arts (unchanged, in a much different way than the modern P. R. C. sport wushu movement). They established the famous Central Martial Arts Institute (Chung Yang Koushu Kuan) in 1928 in the then capitol of Nanjing. Many of the most famous and leading martial artists in China at the time taught there, including: Wan Lai Sheng, Li Jinglin, Fu Chen Sung, Gu Ruzhang, Yang Cheng Fu, Sun Lu Tang and Chen Pan Ling. Many of its graduates went on to become famous living legends, as well; including Chang Tung Sheng and Fu Shu Yun.

At this highly influential institution, they developed and established curricula in the various styles and sub-styles of Chinese martial arts, based upon the characteristics of these styles. Each curriculum/style was headed by a leading Grandmaster (Yang Cheng Fu head of Taiji; Sun Lu Tang head of Xing Yi; Fu Chen Sung, head of Bagua, etc...).

Well, the Chinese Revolution (1945–1949) changed and ended many things, and gave birth to others. One of the things which ended was the Central Koushu Institute at Nanjing. The Guoshu/Koushu people, many of its leaders anyway, were associated with the losing side of the Chinese Revolution (the institute itself was destroyed). Many of these leaders were Generals and military leaders associated with the Nationalist's (the losers of the Revolution), and fled to Taiwan and assisted in the development of the Republic of China there.

After a while they re-established the Kuoshu Arts and Teachings as best as they could there.

Dr. Pai's association with the Koushu Movement took off after the historic visit in 1976 to Taiwan to be tested and perform along with other Koushu Teams. Dr. Pai and his group the "White Dragon Society" earned the "Superb Merit Achievement Award" for their performances.

Program of Koushu Demonstrations, White Dragon Society (Dr. Pai and Team), Taipei, Taiwan, 1976

In 1978 Dr. Pai was appointed "Delegate at Large" of the C.K.W.P.A. and a Vice-President of the C.K.W.P.A. on the 2nd Executive Board Nov. 10, 1983. In 1984 he would go on to become the President and Founder of the "Chinese Koushu Worldwide Promotion Association – U.S.A. Branch." He and his various instructors and those associated with him participated in numerous Koushu World Tourney's; including hosting the historic 1980 3rd World Koushu Tourney in Hawaii (first time not in China) and the 6th World Koushu Tourney in Las Vegas in 1989.

Dr. Daniel K. Pai being carried by the Taiwan Koushu Team at the 3rd World Koushu Games hosted by Dr. Pai in Hawaii, photo courtesy of GM Marcia Pickands

Amongst the many things that happened during the "White Dragon Society's" visit to Taiwan in 1976, Dr. Pai's students were afforded the honor of being allowed to train with Master's and Grandmaster's of the Koushu Federation (as it came to be called). As described to me by my teacher, they were brought to a large open field where various teachers were assembled, and they were allowed to observe the Grandmaster's performing their arts and to choose which one they wanted to learn from. My teacher noticed an elderly master who was performing his movements very slowly like Taiji, then he would explode and do them with speed and power, lightning fast; then go right back to the slow style. Although they spoke different languages, my instructor felt a connection, and he decided this was the teacher he wanted to learn from. This teacher turned out to be Shaolin Grandmaster Wu Jen Dai, a Shaolin disciple who had immigrated to Taiwan around the time of the Revolution to escape persecution and spread his arts in freedom. GM Wu was loosely affiliated with the Koushu Federation (as the C.K. W.P.A. would become known), and was the head of the Shaolin Five Form Fist System, which was one of the official curriculums of the Koushu Federation, R.O.C.

So, my teacher became a lineage disciple of GM Wu, and due to his great discipline and talents, a successor and Headmaster of the Shaolin Five Form Fist System (Wu Xing Quan Fa). When my teacher split from Dr. Pai, this was the lineage he represented publicly and he maintained connections with the Koushu Federation, R.O.C., as a Lifetime Member.

Now, much of the curriculum of Five Form Fist as taught by my teacher comes directly from Dr. Pai's "Pai Lum" system, as it is of such high quality and fits into the overall structure of the art. This includes the "Shaolin Butterfly Style" which within the overall structure of the Five Form Fist Shaolin system is simultaneously an "Internal Style" and a "Southern Shaolin Style" as well as being the "Inner Connector Style" of the entire Five Form Fist System. We will talk about that more and what it means in a subsequent chapter. For now let's briefly examine the structure of the Shaolin Five Form Fist System as a whole, as it is the "Mother System" of the "Shaolin Butterfly Style."

The Butterfly's Mother

The Shaolin Five Form Fist System is composed of 5 main sub-styles, with a 6th major sub-style also contained within it. An entire series of books could be written on this traditional system, here we will just briefly describe it.

The Shaolin Five Form Fist System

Let's examine the sub-styles of the Shaolin Five Form Fist System:

Taiji/Internal Styles

This division of the Five Form fist is a complete system unto itself, as are the other sub-divisions. To the public my teacher taught Yang style Taiji; however contained within the larger division and curriculum are a number of rare Taiji and Internal Styles. One of these is the Shaolin Butterfly Style, a rare Shaolin Internal Style. Other styles preserved here include styles from Dr. Pai's lineage, such as Pai Yueng and Wu Chun Taiji, Daoist Golden Snake, and more.

Sifu Michael Fuchs, Wu Chun Taiji

In the next chapter we will explore what terms like Internal//External mean in more depth.

Southern Shaolin

The Southern Shaolin Division features forms, arts, and methods representative of this broad sub-style of Chinese Martial Arts. As the old kung fu saying puts it, "Hands in the South, Legs in the North." Southern Shaolin styles are characterized by strong, low stances; more hand than leg techniques, including intricate striking and blocking patterns; footwork patterns which move to all directions; and a variety of breathing methods – from smooth and natural to dynamic tension. It is a generally close to mid-range fighting system.

Sifu Michael Fuchs, Dragon Wings

Being a Southern Shaolin System, the Butterfly Style also fits into this sub-division although it is a bit atypical being an Internal Style. Hung Gar and Wing Chun are examples of famous, orthodox Southern Shaolin Styles.

Northern Shaolin

This sub-division of Five Form Fist features classic Northern Shaolin styles, methods, and forms. Northern Shaolin is characterized by long, extended stances; East – West or North – South footwork patterns; high and acrobatic kicking methods combined with low, squatting and spinning methods; smooth, natural breathing; and more leg than hand techniques. Northern Shaolin is a long-range fighting system, primarily. Famous sets here include Ling Po Ch'uan (Lien Bu Quan), Gung Li, Tan Tui, Chang Chuan, and Boc Hoc.

Keep in mind these descriptions are generalities only, exceptions to each exist. For instance, Taiji Quan is a Northern Style, but is much different than Northern Shaolin Crane. Having said that, it must also be remembered that all Chinese systems are more alike than different, branches of the same tree.

Ch'uan Fa (Quan Fa)

This sub-division of the Five Form Fist features numerous self-defense sets. "Ch'uan Fa/Quan Fa" essentially means, "Chinese Way of the Fist." It is analogous to Kenpo/Kempo. The two main systems preserved here are Chinese/Hawaiian Ch'uan Fa and Chinese/Okinawan Ch'uan Fa. These are essentially Chinese styles which were transmitted to other nations/regions, preserved by Dr. Pai and my teacher; which are integral to the Shaolin Five Form Fist System of which he is Headmaster of.

These are very practical and effective methods, which a skilled instructor is able to teach in such a way that the limitations of pre-set self-defense sets are transcended and true, free-style fighting ability is attained.

The Chinese/Hawaiian Ch'uan Fa curriculum contains hundreds of self-defense sets but only one form, an internal monkey set. In "Pai Lum" lineages this curriculum is known as "White Lotus Kempo." One of the Chinese/Okinawan styles famous sets is known as "Chinese Soft Fist."

Chinese Weapons Division

Obviously, each of the previous sub-divisions contains weapons training, forms, and applications. The thing is, however, is that weapons are weapons. It is the weapon itself, along with the culture, geography, laws of the land, and capabilities of the practitioner which dictates how it is used. A person who had never seen them before would soon figure out how to eat food with a fork, spoon, and knife.

So here the student learns about the main classes of Chinese weapons and how they are utilized. The foundational weapons are the Staff/Spear, Saber/Broadsword, and Double-Edged Straight Sword. Some of the main categories of weapons include: rigid weapons, flexible weapons, semi-flexible weapons, and projectile weapons. And, of course, there are weapons for all ranges of combat: from close range Emei Piercers, to Blow Guns and Bow and Arrow (projectile weapons).

Sifu Michael Fuchs with Nine-Section Steel Whip

Now, Shaolin Five Form Fist also has a sixth major division of technique; which is a study unto itself and like Chinese Weapons Study is also found in every other sub-division. This is the study of Chinese Chin-na/Gao Ti (Grappling) Methods. This division contains numerous simple to complex methods, applications, and forms. For instance, Taiji Na Fa is quite distinct from Tiger Style Chin-na. The basic method is known as "Five Star Chin-na." Entire styles are contained here, such as Crown Eagle Chin-na, a high achievement and system of two-person fighting sets which emphasize chin-na grips and escapes.

Chin-na focuses on methods of seizing, controlling, interrupting and rupturing the joints, blood, and breath. Gao Ti/Grappling is a broader category of combat which includes all manner of holds, sweeps, takedowns, and groundwork. Shuai-jiao is an example of a more modern style of Chinese grappling art.

So, as you can see, the Shaolin Five Form Fist is a huge system. The Shaolin Butterfly Style is the "hidden jewel" at the very center of the system. I must say, I am in awe of what my teacher was able to accomplish in the field of Asian martial arts and especially in inheriting and developing this awesome system. This book represents an attempt to preserve one aspect of it, the rare Shaolin Butterfly Style, in written form.

Now, another way to view and organize the Shaolin Five Form Fist System is through the lens of Chinese Animal Styles. The main ones here being the famous Shaolin Five Animals— Tiger, Leopard, Snake, Crane, and Dragon. Two other important animal (insect) sub-styles in our system are the Monkey and the Butterfly. In the next chapter we will explore the concept and application of Animal Styles and Xing/Hsing (Form/Shape) more, as well as various other concepts important to understanding the Shaolin Butterfly Style.

Chapter Two: Kung Fu Essentials

As mentioned in chapter one, the Shaolin Butterfly Style is a "High, Internal Style" of Chinese martial arts. But what does that mean? Let's explore these concepts now, as well as others which are important to understanding the Shaolin Butterfly Style. These concepts are fundamental to viewing and understanding martial arts in general, as well.

Kung Fu-ology

Chinese martial arts are the most sophisticated, comprehensive, and deepest systems in existence. They have been in continuous practice and refinement since Stone Age times, beginning in ancient China 7,000 years ago; and eventually world-wide. So naturally, there are and have been quite a few terms in use to describe them.

"Kung Fu" is a term synonymous with martial arts, especially in the West. However "Kung Fu" technically speaking does not refer to martial arts practice and skills alone ("Kung Fu" is also known as "gong fu", "gung fu," and "kang-hu").

"Kung" refers to work, achievement, and merit. "Fu" refers to time and effort. Put together the words describe skills which have been gained through practice, time and discipline/effort. Thus "Kung Fu" can be used to describe a wide variety of skills and achievements. Due to his legendary practice, workout regimens, and study of the game the NBA great Larry Bird could be described as having great "Kung Fu" with basketball. His basketball "Kung Fu" permeated every aspect of the game as well; as he won titles not only as an Olympian and NBA player, but as a Head Coach and NBA Team Executive.

The "Kung Fu" aspect of martial arts practice was one my teacher emphasized, utilizing many real-life examples to describe it to us. Truly, one can have "Kung Fu" in so many aspects of life: we can be "Kung Fu" cooks, teachers, programmers, musicians, Fathers, ditch-diggers, or what have you. Even Teenage Mutant Ninja Turtles can have "Kung Fu" – cowabunga!

This term came to be associated with Chinese martial arts as the arts spread West-ward, no doubt as Chinese speakers explained to non-Chinese speakers that this or that particular practitioner of the arts had "good Kung Fu." Not knowing any better the non-Chinese speakers just associated it with the practice of martial arts in general.

There is also a Chinese term which utilizes "Kung Fu" to specifically refer to Chinese martial arts, that being "kung fu wushu."

Other terms utilized to describe Chinese martial arts include "Quan Shu" (Ch'uan Shu), meaning "martial/fist arts" and "Quan Fa" (Ch'uan Fa) meaning the "martial/fist way and techniques." "Quan" or "Ch'uan" is very specialized in its use in martial arts, meaning more like the "fist within the fist," or the "mysterious fist" and is a symbol for Chinese martial arts as a whole. "Fa" means the way, not as in "The Way" or "Dao," but as in the proper technique and way of training, practicing, and performing a skill or art. On his hilarious cooking and travel show, *No Reservations*, I remember seeing the late and inimitable Anthony Bourdain in one episode visiting the various regions of China, sampling the food and culture. In one bit he visited a traditional calligraphy master to receive a lesson. The first character he was assigned was "Fa." Being a true master, the calligrapher was imparting multiple lessons all at once, beyond merely brushing lines on a piece of paper. Similarly, the first lesson in all of our martial arts (as taught by my teacher) is the Ceremonial Bow, which contains the entire art in a seed form. With all true masters the first lessons are the most important, pay attention!

"Wuyi" meaning "martial arts" is another term which was popular for centuries to describe Chinese martial arts in its pure sense as methods of combat. In recent times the term "wushu" has been widely utilized, meaning "martial arts" but with a more sportive and performance arts flavor. On Taiwan (The Republic of China) the term "guoshu/koushu" is common, meaning "national arts." This is similar to how here in the U.S. baseball is referred to as "the national past-time." "Guoshu/Koushu" traces its usage to the deposed Kuomintang government and the Central Martial Arts Institute (Chung Yang Koushu Kuan), established in 1928 in Nanjing.

Another term which is often utilized to refer to martial arts in general, especially here in the U.S., is "Karate." "Karate" was born in Okinawa, and originally referred to the "Chinese Hand" meaning Chinese martial arts ("Kara" meaning China and "Te" hand). The meaning was changed by the great Master Gichin Funakushi when "Karate" was introduced to the Japanese school system. The characters utilized were changed from those meaning "Kara – Chinese" and "Te – hand" to "Kara – empty" and "Te – hand." "Empty" thus referring to the Buddhist concept of Shunyata, or emptiness/void. So, using the term "Karate" to refer to Chinese martial arts is no less legitimate than "kung fu;" perhaps more so.

There are many other terms in use for Chinese martial arts as well, including to describe specialties, such as "shuai jiao" for Chinese wrestling. These are the main ones, however.

Shapes and Forms

Chinese martial arts are famous for their "animal" and "elemental" styles. There are numerous styles named for animals, insects, fish, and even mythical creatures; such as the Dragon, Phoenix, and Roc. The animals/creatures are utilized as a symbol for the style due to the importance of its influence on its technique and various other reasons. The study of Mother Nature and her creatures is a key component of traditional martial arts training. In a similar way, there are also styles which incorporate the use of natural elements in their practice and application. Such as the use of the "5 Elements" famous in Daoist philosophy, cosmology, and medicine: Earth, Water, Metal, Fire, and Wood. Other natural elements include lightning, thunder and clouds.

The Shaolin Butterfly Style is one of these, in this case an "insect style." The Butterfly is an earthly symbol of beauty and transformation, which are concepts important to the style. The Butterfly Wings come together to form a shape which is similar to the "Infinity Symbol" ∞, another important symbol for the style. In a later chapter we will discuss this in depth.

The Chinese word which describes the use of these creatures/elements in the context of martial arts is "Xing (hsing)" which simply means "shape" or "form." My teacher's art in Chinese is thus "Shaolin Wu Xing Quan-fa." Another famous art which utilizes both animal and elemental "xing" is called "Xing-I Quan-fa," or "Form and Will Martial Art."

In addition to styles, numerous techniques and forms take their name from an "animal" or "elemental" "Xing." Such as the "ram's head punch" "the willow palms" the "metal punch" and "Taming the Tiger," a famous Hung Gar set.

Levels of "Xing" Training

There are three main levels to the study of "Xing" in martial arts, which can be applied to Form, Technique, and Application.

1.Fitness:

The first level is to develop the strength, fitness, endurance and flexibility to attempt to perform the techniques/forms ("Xing") properly. For new students this can be quite a significant hurdle, even for the young and healthy. Attempting to perform techniques patterned after Tigers and Leopards, Monkey's and Snakes, Crane's and Elephants – and so many others – is among the most rigorous and difficult physical training there is, bar none. Chinese martial arts are not only beautiful, they require speed and power, extreme dexterity and coordination, changes in energy and tempo, great suppleness and flexibility, and more. It can take one to three years get into proper condition to perform Chinese martial arts well.

Many a student falls by the wayside at this level.

2. Perform with Skill and Accuracy:

Once the first hurdle has been cleared, the student focuses on performing the forms and techniques as perfectly possible. Having a skilled and experienced instructor is key here. Techniques such as "tiger claw" "leopard fist" "crane's wings" the "tiger leap" and the "dragon's tail" will not work unless they are formed properly and utilized skillfully. This includes conditioning, such as iron hand/fist/body. Again, properly and safely, which is where having a skilled and experienced instructor is most important.

Traditional Chinese martial arts are quite sophisticated and can be beautiful to watch; but we must remember, unlike modern sport wushu they are not designed to be performance arts. It isn't a game or a show. Most styles require mastery of internal and external methods which can take years to develop in order to be practical and effective. One of the old teachings is, "ten years to basic level of mastery." And that is only for someone taught properly and who has trained hard daily.

3. Internalize the Essence:

This level comes only after many years of practice. Getting in shape and perfecting the technique (levels one and two) is mainly the practice of the "outer form/xing." The use of the "dragon claw" "crane's talons" and the "earth fist" and "lightning hands" has more to it than just how one forms the technique, breathes, steps, deflects, and strikes. The essence, energy, and spirit of these techniques is different. This is the level of the "inner xing." One must sincerely practice and live the arts, study the animal or element in Nature, and allow it to settle into one's heart to achieve this high level. This is the level of mastery of one's art, and is similar to a martial style of "shamanism."

My teacher's teacher, Dr. Daniel K. Pai, was simply referred to by his students as "Lung," or when he was older, "Lao Lung," – the Dragon or wise, old Dragon. My teacher told me that what separated him from the rest and made him so special was that he had totally perfected and mastered a technique and skill known as "the Dragon's Tail." Doing so entails much more than the words imply, and results in a multitude of skills. One of the traditional arts he inherited and was the grandmaster of is known as "Pai Te Lung" or the strong, pure, and virtuous White Dragon. For all intents and purposes he was thus a "Human Dragon" and was recognized as such.

The famous grandmaster, Paulie Zink, also exemplifies this, as a living human "monkey." He is a monkey stylist at a very high level, he even eats a diet similar to what a monkey eats.

The old saying "it can take ten years to become a real student" gives one the idea of what kind of sincerity and discipline is needed to approach this level. Are you a real student? Then keep after it!

Internal – External

As previously stated, the Shaolin Butterfly style is a "High, Internal" style of Chinese martial arts. Now that we have explored the practice and the concept of "Xing" a bit, let's examine what the terms "High" and "Internal" and related terms mean in the context of Chinese martial arts.

"Internal" is often utilized interchangeably with the term "soft," and the same goes for "External" and "hard style." However, they all convey unique meanings.

Internal
(Soft, Esoteric)

External
(Hard, Exoteric)

The Horizontal Continuum of Styles

Additionally, their meanings may differ depending on the lineage and style/system we are talking about. For instance "Internal" and "Soft" in Yang style Taiji is quite different than how they are understood in Japanese Goju Ryu Karate, both in practice and application. The same can be said regarding "External" and "Hard." What's "Soft and Internal" in one style may be the opposite in another and vice-versa. It's all relative. In general, Chinese styles are all to Internal/Soft side compared to Okinawan, Japanese and most other orthodox Karate styles (a broad generalization, there are numerous exceptions – such as Filipino kali and Japanese aikido, both being "Internal/Soft" Styles).

> What we are specifically referring to here are the <u>Training Methods</u>, <u>Martial Applications</u>, and <u>Martial Styles</u> in general.

In Chinese styles the meaning of an "Internal Style" is exemplified by the old Daoist teaching of the "soft overcoming the hard" as far as martial technique goes. Taiji methods of receiving, passing, neutralizing, re-directing, and issuing force exemplify this style. Circular and spiral force is emphasized.

As far as training methods go "Internal" styles will utilize the following:

- Natural breathing as well as "inner breathing" methods which emphasize the lower "dan-tien" or "energy field/zone."

- Utilizing the inner parts of ourselves in a coordinated way to maximize efficiency and power with a minimum of effort – internal energy, fluids, connective tissues, tendons, ligaments, and the heart/mind/intent/awareness.
- The faculties of the mind, heart, imagination, and visualization – along with sound – will be utilized.

Together these are known as the "Three Regulations (San Tiao)" though perhaps "Three Harmonizations" is a better term.

The "Bamboo Legs" exercise and "Bamboo" training in general are well known examples of "Internal" training methods. "Bamboo Training" leads to a supple, pliable body and efficient body mechanics and technique. These are, of course, important both for health and longevity, as well as efficient and powerful martial techniques.

As the Sage Lao Tzu put it long ago,

"Nothing under heaven is softer or more yielding than water; but when it attacks things hard and resistant there is not one of them that can prevail. That the yielding conquers the resistant and the soft conquers the hard is a fact known by all men, yet utilized by none."

-Dao De Jing, chapter 78

Famous "Internal Styles" include Taiji Quan, Xing-I Quan, Bagua Zhang, Liu Ho Ba Fa, the Bando Monk style, and Aikido. Due to its training methods and progression the Shaolin Butterfly Style is also an "Internal Style." The modern description of "Wudang Styles" as being "Internal" and "Shaolin Styles" as being "External" is misleading and inaccurate. It has to do with many Chinese believing that "pure Chinese" styles – uninfluenced by outside teachings, such as Indian teachings mixed with the native Chinese at Shaolin – are the "Internal" styles – they come from inside China (such as Wudang/Daoist Styles). Everything else is "External." The fact of the matter is that all of these styles have inter-mixed and knowledge has been exchanged for centuries. But this is a huge topic for another book.

Soft Styles

The term "soft" is often utilized inter-changeably with "Internal" but is also somewhat unique in describing the martial arts. "Soft Styles" are those which emphasize the yin, quietude, going with, passivity, evasion and countering, or containing and controlling the opponent's force (as in utilizing grips, holds, and locks of various kinds). They are generally more defensive in nature, favoring non-lethal methods.

> "Soft Style does not mean slow and feeble. It does not mean small and weak in structure. Practitioners of the Soft Style may be physically strong, fast in movement, mentally alert and highly skillful in the martial arts. Because of religious, moral and ethical principles, they employ techniques of controlled force to minimize injury to the opponents."
> -Dr. Maung Gyi, Bando, *Philosophy, Principles, and Practice: An Overview of the FREE-HAND Systems*

"Soft" may also be utilized to describe training methods, such as the "soft iron palm" or "cotton palm" training. This one, in classic Daoist fashion, leads from very soft to extremely hard (within the soft) and powerful though this will take years to achieve. My teacher utilized a combination of "soft" and "hard" methods to achieve a body that was like the classic "iron wrapped in cotton." His bones became 10x thicker than the average human male (his entire skeleton was x-rayed by his chiropractor, who was quite perplexed by this). Guess what getting hit by him was like? Ouch! And forget striking him and hurting him – unless you had a 10 gauge shot gun.

Another term utilized alongside "Internal" and "Soft" is "Esoteric." An "Esoteric Style" is one which is hidden and secret.

This may be literal, like how the Shaolin Butterfly Style used to be, not to be shown or talked about in public ever. Or it may be "hidden in plain sight" such as Taiji Quan. Most people viewing Taiji would never be able to fathom the power it contains. This is true of all Chinese Kung Fu styles actually, contained within the techniques and forms there are numerous "secrets." The art being like an unlimited, buried treasure – the more you dig (practice) the more there is.

To the beginner, learning to make a circle with the hand is simple – make a circle, "big deal." To a true expert with decades of experience the Circle is a magical technique, with limitless "points" and applications. So train hard and study well.

External Styles

The "External Style" in application is exemplified by "force vs. force" technique; especially what is known as "collision force technique" – like rams butting heads in the Spring-time.

The bigger, harder, faster force wins. Linear and square force is emphasized. Hard, right-angle blocks and direct, aggressive striking methods are featured.

The breathing methods utilized include forced and tensed "unnatural methods;" such as dynamic tension and the famous Japanese "ibuki" breathing. The muscles of the body will be utilized in a tense/relax fashion, with segmented power being utilized at times. Training will emphasize very rigorous physical activity, speed, power, and explosive movements. There will be heavy physical contact right from the start, with body conditioning and "tempering" being emphasized.

As an example the first "kick defense" I learned in our Shaolin System (like in the first class I took) was to stand in a bow and arrow stance with my hands behind my back while an experienced, hard as nails Sifu delivered flying side-kicks to my abdomen! Before the flying side-kicks commenced he used his hands and feet in a somewhat more gentle fashion to show me how to properly use my breath, body, posture, and stance to safely receive the force. This was done by slapping, striking, kicking, sweeping and even climbing onto me. Then he just let fly with the flying sidekicks (bouncing off me each time).

As "receiving force" is a key skill in martial arts (without being injured or uprooted) I have always been grateful to this teacher for this important lesson. Regardless of style, "receiving force" is essential. One must be able to "receive" the force fully – without fear – in order to properly re-direct, manage, or control it.

Famous Chinese "External Styles" include Hung Gar, Shaolin Tiger and Leopard, Lohan, and Longfist. Shaolin styles are generally referred to as "External Styles" though this is misleading. Shaolin contains numerous "Internal Styles" and training methods. The Shaolin Butterfly Style being one. Grandmaster Wong Kiew Kit has done a wonderful job illustrating this in his books on Shaolin Kung Fu, Qi Gong and Chan/Zen.

Chinese styles, in general, are all to the "Internal/Soft" end of the spectrum compared to orthodox Korean, Okinawan, and Japanese styles of Karate.

Hard Styles

So, the "Hard Style" arts will feature explosive speed and power, violent offensive techniques which target vital areas, killing blows, breaking of bones and joints, and body conditioning methods. To quote the immortal "Cobra Kai" of "Karate Kid" fame – they show "no mercy!"

The term "Exoteric Style" is also utilized to describe arts of the "External/Hard" school. My teacher earned a black belt from the legendary "Godhand" Mas Oyama, in 1966. Back then this was an almost impossible feat, only 3 of 45 passed this test; his black belt was like number 125 out of tens of thousands of Oyama students world-wide. He told me that Oyama had such obvious, fear-some power that when he threw his infamous reverse punch, you didn't want to be within 25 feet of it! The dojo walls shook from the power.

So, the "External/Hard/Exoteric" school is like a ravenous, hunting tiger – only a fool would dare approach. The "Internal/ Soft/Esoteric" school is like the small and beautiful Coral snake. Seemingly weak and harmless, but containing a poison so lethal it can kill a bull elephant with one bite, instantly.

Training in either school can be extremely painful and challenging. Do not let the term "soft" fool you. Try holding a single posture unmoving for one hour at a time (a common training method of the "Internal" school). Just imagine the strength and inner harmony/connections which come from this when done daily for many years, combined with other training methods.

"There are many styles of Chinese martial arts. After the Sui (589–618 AD) and Tang (618–907 AD) dynasties, they were divided into two schools: shaolin and wutang. Within these two schools, there are further divisions. We speak of Shaolin as external style and wutang as internal style. Others say Shaolin is hard style (wai kung), and wutang is soft style (nei kung). In any case, because they are arts of combat, Chinese martial arts must contain both soft and hard techniques so that they can encompass both defense and offense. The only difference between Shaolin and wutang is the method of training students. Shaolin starts with hard strokes, but wutang begins with soft ones. Shaolin goes from hard to soft, and wutang is the opposite. It goes from soft to hard. The final goal for both styles is the same: to train people to use a combination of soft and hard strokes to fight."[3]

So, the key for any serious student of martial arts is *BALANCE*. This balance is needed for two main reasons – *Combat Necessity and Effectiveness* and *Longevity – Spirit, Mind, Body*. If we stray and stay too far in any direction we risk becoming unbalanced in our training, and in life – thus we would be weakening our art and ourselves, rather than vitalizing.

---

3   Chen Pan Ling, Chen Pan Ling's Original Tai Chi Chuan Textbook (Blitz Design), 4–5.

Students should find a true Master/Teacher and follow their instructions to the letter. There are many, so many, phonies and "YouTube grandmasters" out there now. Be well and beware.

High and Low

High Styles

Low Styles

So, the division of Internal/External styles of martial arts represents the horizontal continuum. The vertical continuum of the arts is symbolized by the division of the "High Styles" and the "Low Styles."

As I have been taught, there are three main features which differentiate whether a style is a "High" or a "Low" style, or somewhere in the middle.

1. Emotional Discipline
2. Technique Utilized
3. Intent and Objective

The famous quote from Master Kan of the classic T.V. show "Kung Fu" is a perfect description of the "High Style":

"Perceive the way of nature and no force of man can harm you. Do not meet a wave head on: avoid it. You do not have to stop force: it is easier to redirect it. Learn more ways to preserve rather than destroy. Avoid rather than check. Check rather than hurt. Hurt rather than maim. Maim rather than kill. For all life is precious nor can any be replaced."

-Master Kan,

fictional Abbot of the Shaolin Monastery from the classic "Kung Fu" T.V. show

So a "High Style" is often one taught with a spiritual intent, with character development and even the achievement of self-realization being the goal of training. This was exactly how we were taught. My teacher's school and our symbol was the "White Lotus" one of the symbols of enlightenment found all over Asia. Classes were conducted in a temple-like atmosphere, meditative discipline was expected no matter how intense the training was. We were taught that "love is our shield, knowledge is our sword."

Practitioners of the "High Style" exhibit grace under pressure, without sacrificing awareness or safety. Technically, they prefer evasion, redirection, and non-lethal methods (such as controlling, unbalancing, and pain compliance techniques). They will receive and bear pain and suffering without retaliating if this is a viable option.

Examples of the "High Style" include the Shaolin Butterfly Style and Shaolin Five Form Fist in general, Temple Style Taiji, Aikido, and the Bando Monk Style.

The "Low Style" is the opposite of all of this. Practitioners train in an atmosphere of pain, aggression, rage, violence, and hate. The ego predominates over all. This style was immortalized in the classic movie "The Karate Kid" (the original), with the portrayal of the "Cobra Kai" and their cult-like leader and his cruel motto "No Mercy!" Although it might seem a bit "hokey" I encourage all to see this movie and absorb the lessons it imparts. Kudos to the writer, Robert Mark Kamen, and to technical director Grandmaster Pat Johnson for pouring their hearts into this great movie.

So "Low Style" practitioners will train with negative, unchecked emotions, emphasize techniques which are violent and injure, even causing death in extreme cases. The intent is to cause pain and suffering. The slightest real or imagined provocation will be met with a massively over-the-top response. There is nothing too barbaric for the worst of these types, including genocide, rape, torture, and the like. The Nazis under Hitler's "leadership" and ISIS exemplify the lowest of the "Low Style."

Internal/External, High/Low

Now, of course, all of these approaches to the arts can be, and are, inter-mixed in a myriad of ways.

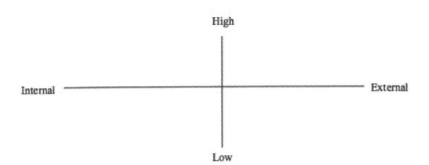

So we have "High, Internal" styles, such as the Shaolin Butterfly Style, Temple Style Taiji, Aikido, and the Bando Monk System. "High, External" styles would be Shaolin systems such as Hung Gar which retain the Shaolin ethics, or karate styles which are taught in the manner portrayed by "Mr. Miyagi" of "Karate Kid" fame. The "High, External" style is also featured at well run tourneys and fighting matches. No matter the level of contact the rules are followed and respect is maintained at all times, especially towards the judges and fellow competitors.

An example of an "Internal, Low" style would be the application of police/law enforcement tactics here in the U.S.A. The intent is to cause minimal (or no) harm, but the practitioner's (police/security forces) may have little emotional control due to limited training.

The "Low/External" style is typified by active duty military combatants, the intent being in all-out war to destroy the enemy. Soldiers may be dominated by fear, confusion, high anxiety, anger, worry, and similar emotional states. Note that even here – warfare – rules have been worked out in modern times regarding the use of force which virtually all modern militaries follow. Only a few rogue states led by evil dictators and terror groups flout these rules; such as minimizing harm to civilians, not using chemical weapons, and the like.

Kung Fu Roots

The ultimate and most vital "Kung Fu Root" is the foundation, development, and application of "stance." Quite simply, No Stance = No Kung Fu, as well as No Stance = No Power/ Gong. This goes not only for the Shaolin Butterfly Style, but Chinese styles in general; as well as most classical styles of Korean, Okinawan, and Japanese Karate (amongst others, such as Burmese Bando and Vietnamese Styles). By "stance" we are referring to the various configurations of the legs that we stand upon – with both feet touching the earth, as well as single leg stances.

The key Root/Mother Stance is the famous "Horse Stance." The various styles will utilize differing versions of this bedrock stance – some higher, some lower; some wider, some narrower – but they will all emphasize the "Horse." The basic idea is like it sounds – the feet and legs are spread apart as if riding a horse. In many systems, including the Shaolin Butterfly Style, the most basic "horse stance" is the double-shoulder width, thighs parallel with the ground, "horse" known as "sei ping dai ma."

Practicing and developing this low and wide horse stance does much more than build strong legs, it is truly the foundation of all other techniques – as well as breath, power, and health and longevity. Combined with proper breathing methods the "qi" is developed in the lower "dan-tien (energy zone)" and the power of the legs becomes united and developed ("dang ging"). As the old saying puts it, "a horse stance a day keeps the doctor away."

The "horse stance" is so important in Chinese martial arts that its Chinese term "ma" or "horse" is synonymous with all other stances, which are thought of as variations of the basic "horse stance." In the Shaolin Five Form Fist System some of the main stances utilized include: horse stance, bow and arrow stance, cat stance, false stance, cross stance, crane stance, rear bow stance, side bow stance, spinning top stance, twisted stance, monkey stance, ready stance, hour-glass stance, san-ti stance, and many others.

The stances themselves are also techniques utilized in combat applications, generally combined with the use of the hands. For instance, at close-range the "horse stance" is quite effective to utilize in order to trip-up and takedown an opponent. The "cat stance" not only aids in developing balance, mobility, and agility; it serves as a foundation for numerous kicking and leg maneuvers. The "crane stance" obviously builds balance and strength while standing on one leg – but it may also be utilized to break an opponent's arm or deflect his kick.

Stance training generally begins with static stance training; holding the stances while otherwise motionless while the hands/arms are formed in various postures. From here the student proceeds to "moving stance-work." The student then proceeds to moving through the stances slowly and meticulously, up to full running speed (as in "dragon walking" methods). At a certain point this "moving stance training" will transform into "footwork" training. Most classical Chinese, Korean, Okinawan, and Japanese styles will begin with "stance training" rather than the quicker moving "footwork training." We will discuss "footwork training" in a bit.

One final thought on "stances." No matter how long one trains, one will always need to practice stance training. A student asked the famous Taiji Grandmaster Cheng Man Ching, "when will my legs stop hurting?" His answer was, "when you stop training." Keep after it!

Another key "Kung Fu Root" is known as "Posture." "Posture" refers to the various configurations of the torso, arms/hands, and head – from the waist up. The Shaolin Butterfly Style, due to its emphasis on joined wrist/palm methods has a variety of unique postures which are generally not seen in other styles. These will be detailed in a later chapter.

"Posture" and "Stance" are generally combined in a student's basic training, as in holding a stance and forming the arms/hands into various positions. One of the basic methods in Five Form Fist Shaolin is to stand in a "bow and arrow stance" and form the arms into the "five-star guard."

Generally, people will refer to a single combination of a stance and a posture as a "posture." Such as the postures which make up a form (kuen/kata). However, technically speaking, "stance" refers to the waist down, and "posture" to the waist and above. From Novice up to Intermediate Level the various stances and postures will generally always be practiced the same way. As one approaches Expert/Master Level, they may be changed and mixed and matched as needed.

An example of this being the Yang Style Taiji "Single Whip Posture," which is generally practiced in the Taiji version of a bow and arrow stance. However, other stances may be utilized while forming this famous posture, such as a "cross stance." Doing so alters the martial application, as needed. Any single stance may serve as the foundation for numerous "postures."

A key feature of "stance training" and "postures" is learning to both receive force from any direction and to be able to project force into any direction – in each and every stance/posture (N, S, E, W, NW, NE, SW, SE). Additionally, the power and functionality of the "central line (zhong ding)" must be built into every stance/posture.

Stance/Posture in Chinese martial arts is similar in many ways to the concept and practice of "asana" in Indian Hatha Yoga. The difference being, of course, that the "martial dimension" is added to the stretching, strengthening, breathing, and shamanic type applications of "asana."

So, as you can see, the history, development, and practice of stance and posture in the Asian martial arts is very deep. This is merely an introduction to a vital element of the Shaolin Butterfly Style.

More Kung Fu Roots

"Body Mechanics – The application of physical principles to achieve maximum efficiency and to limit risk of physical stress or injury to the practitioner of physical therapy, massage therapy, chiropractic or osteopathic manipulation."

*-Medical Dictionary for the Health
Professions and Nursing*

"Body Mechanics – Systemic exercises designed especially to develop coordination, endurance, and poise."

-Merriam – Webster Dictionary

As one can see from the above definitions, a key aspect of the practice of Asian martial arts – including the Shaolin Butterfly Style – is the development of proper body mechanics. Added to these descriptions, in the case of martial arts, is its importance in executing all aspects of the martial arts, including the combat applications. My teacher described it this way:

"Footwork represents the large-frame (macrocosm) of movement in the martial arts; and body mechanics represents the small-frame (microcosm)."
                -Tao Chi Li, Shaolin Five Form Fist Headmaster

The development of proper body mechanics in martial arts rests upon the foundation of proper stance, posture, breathing, eye focus, inner alignment, mind/body coordination, and more. Stance, posture, and body mechanics serve as a foundation for footwork, which we will explore coming up.

Keep in mind this discussion of body mechanics is meant merely as an introduction to an important topic. Entire books could be written on any one of these "Kung Fu Roots."

Body mechanics development and application in Asian martial arts is generally much deeper an art than is seen in say, massage therapy, physical therapy, or even in the various dance disciplines. Asian martial arts have been in continuous development for thousands of years, along with their African, Middle Eastern, and Indian cousins – which are also quite ancient. Nowadays martial arts from all over planet Earth are interfacing and intermixing, leading to a great explosion of knowledge (if not always quality).

One of the specific ways body mechanics in martial arts is unique compared to other arts is that it is meant to be effective in order to maximize the ability to receive force, control force, and project force – from all directions, one or more opponents, and whether armed/unarmed.

Various martial arts systems will employ differing methods of body mechanics and other methods whose development depends upon the Culture, Environment, Technology, and Government they were born in/under. Martial arts systems developed in the tribal, blade orientated cultures of the Philippine jungles will naturally be different than those of the Mongolian plains.

In the Shaolin Five Form Fist System there are numerous methods of body mechanics which are developed and employed. Some of the main ones include:

- Bamboo
- Wave
- Weight Shift
- Shoulder Twist

In our internal styles, both "pulling silk" and "reeling silk" styles are utilized.

The basic type of "body mechanics" initially emphasized in the Shaolin Butterfly Style is the "pulling silk" method. "Pulling silk" refers to pulling raw silk off a spool. This must be done with a very smooth, even flowing motion, lest the silk thread be broken. This skill is developed by properly practicing the basic methods for a long enough time; as well as through proper practice of the first form, the "Butterfly Energy Form." Hands-on guidance from a skilled teacher is also essential.

Body mechanics in martial arts entails more than mere muscular and other physical manipulations. It goes deeper, utilizing the breath, awareness, and various meditative methods (nei gong/qi gong) in order to develop specialized applications of power/force/energy. This energy development in Chinese martial arts is known as "gong/gung/kung," which in application is known as "jing/ging." The very energy of life, mind, and body is refined in order to enhance martial power, technique, and skill.

"Float like a butterfly, sting like a bee."

-Muhammad Ali

"Footwork" as the word suggests, refers to various methods of agilely moving, walking, and running. As ones application of "moving in stances" becomes more natural, fluid, and effortless it transforms into, "footwork." Alternatively, certain systems begin with footwork training, such as pekiti-tirsia kali. Mobility is essential due to the bladed combat orientation of the art.

The words of pekiti-tirsia kali Supreme Tuhon Leo T. Gaje, Jr. still ring in my ears:

"In the pekiti-tirsia system we have no blocks! We have no stances! And we have no forms!"

He screamed this at us while drilling us and wielding a whip, in order to emphasize his "point!"

In the Five Form Fist Shaolin System, of which the Shaolin Butterfly Style is the "inner connector style" of – there are numerous footwork methods. Some of the basic ones include:

- Step and slide
- Scooting
- Crossing
- Rising step
- Sinking step
- Squatting step
- Spinning step
- Tiger leap
- Monkey step
- Circle step
- Dragon Walk

In addition to the many basic footwork methods and those developed and introduced in forms, two entire footwork systems are preserved: The Lotus Stepping Footwork System, and the Dragon Walking Footwork System. The Shaolin Butterfly Style techniques work especially well with the Lotus Stepping Methods. The basic concept of the "Lotus Step" is moving the feet in patterns similar to the petal of a lotus flower (semi-circle). The basic methods are the "single lotus step" and the "double lotus step." There are many others, as well, including unique two-person "lotus stepping" push-hands drills and applications (tui shou and san shou).

Lotus Stepping Pattern
"Kung Fu is what you do, Taiji is who you are."
-old kung fu wisdom

Integral to all of these "Kung Fu Roots" are various concepts which are applied to our training in order to guide it properly. Such as "in motion find stillness, in stillness find motion." This leads to a balanced and harmonious state of mind, body, and awareness at all times and has many applications.

Another is "from formlessness to form, from form to formlessness." This describes the path one follows in training from novice student to intermediate level, to expert/mastery level. The beginner has no "form" due to lack of training. Over time with good teaching and hard work the student develops good "form." In fact the best teachers will demand perfection of their students and push them to strive to achieve it. Then, over many years as "form" is perfected, at a true mastery level, it may be relaxed or even discarded. The art has become so natural that any and every thought, movement, and action is an extension of one's art. It is then a true "life art."

The famous aikido 10th Dan Koichi Tohei would say, "if I can raise my hand in perfect harmony with all of the laws of the universe just once, then my practice is done." This is the naturalness we must aspire to.

There are numerous examples of experts who have achieved this level. The famous son of Yang Lu Chan, founder of the Yang Style of Taiji, Yang Chien Hou was once attacked by an expert swordsman while he was sipping tea in his study. Naturally and effortlessly he utilized his feather duster to defeat his armed attacker!

As the legendary "sword saint" Miyamoto Musashi put it, "my fighting step is my walking step, my walking step is my fighting step." He also would fight duels with live-blade (katana sword) wielding opponents and defeat them with a carved piece of wood.

One of my teacher's favorite old kung fu sayings describes the end result of "form to formlessness" very well:

"The neophyte flails his arms and legs with great abandon and energy yet accomplishes little. The Master points his finger and the mountains tremble."

Essentially, all movements are either Natural, Unnatural or Practiced Natural. Natural movements are very few, what we are born with; such as reaching for food or scratching an itch. Everything else is an Unnatural Movement – trying shoelaces, driving a car, martial arts – on and on. With practice, over time, these Unnatural Movements become Practiced Natural Movements. The "form" has become "formless."

A butterfly, of course, was at one time a moth. After its metamorphosis within the cocoon it emerges as a completely new and beautiful creature. This is also another way to symbolize the journey of "form to formless." The Shaolin Butterfly Style is not a "beginner style." It is generally taught to people who already have years of experience in the Shaolin Five Form Fist System, in order to perfect and enhance their skills and abilities and to connect all together. It is a style that will aid in taking those with good form to the next level, "formlessness." Enjoy the journey.

Zoned Out

Some other important "Kung Fu Roots" include the concept, practice, and application of *Angle, Range,* and *Zone.*

"Angle" refers to the orientation between oneself and the environment, including an opponent. Various martial art systems will utilize differing methods of conceptualizing and teaching "Angle."

In the Shaolin Five Form Fist System the most prevalent one utilized is known as the "8 Directions." Where one stands in the center and the "8 Directions" are the 8 main points on the compass – N, S, E, W, NE, NW, SW, SE. The actual central standing position may be thought of as the "9th Direction" one which moves with us as we move and from which the other "8 Directions" emanate from and intersect (through our spine, or "central line").

The development and practice of "Angle" is an essential and deep art which enhances and perfects all technique. It is one of the ways true martial arts experts recognize each other, as a true expert will have a very highly developed and keen sense of "Angle" and a powerfully developed, laser-like "central line."

There are numerous methods of practicing and developing the "8 Directions" including solo, partnered, unarmed, and armed (staff/spear, saber, sword, others) methods. These include the "8 Direction Stepping" methods and various "Lotus Stepping" methods.

Another well-known teaching and practice of "Angle" is the Taiji "Five Directions." The "Five Directions" is essentially a simplification of the "8 Directions" boiling it down to 5: the space in front of us, the space behind us, the space to the left, the space to the right, and the Center – where we are standing. This center in Chinese arts is known as "Central Equilibrium" or "Zhong Ding."

"Zone" refers to the space between 2 Angles, such as the space between N and NE. Angle and Zone are important in honing our skills of Attack and Defense, and are useful in safely navigating the "battlefields" of daily life as well – be it at home, on the road, at work, or in the mall.

"Range" refers to the distance between oneself and one's opponent. Again, there are a variety of methods of determining and categorizing, "Range." In the Shaolin Five Form Fist System and the Shaolin Butterfly Style we define "Range" this way:

Long Range – the range one is at if one stretches one's foot out to full extension forward to touch an opponent while leaning backwards – or the same stretching forward to touch with the hand.

Medium Range – the range one is at if one can stretch the hand out without reaching/leaning and easily touch the opponent.

Close Range – close range refers to the range from being able to touch with the elbow up to full body on body touching.

A skilled martial artist must know how to fight and defend in all of these Ranges and in a variety of ways. They are each a specialization of martial arts training. "Close Range" is often erroneously called "Grappling Range" – the fact is there are specialized Close Range striking methods, both armed and unarmed. It isn't strictly grappling only range.

"Close Range" may be further sub-divided into 5 Inside Ranges:

5. Fingers/Hand

4. Wrist

3. Elbow

2. Shoulder

1. Spine

This configuration of "Range" is especially useful in Chin-Na and Grappling Arts.

Obviously, if weapons are added into the mix then this all changes. Long Range with a long bow or rifle is quite different than with the legs/body alone.

The Shaolin Butterfly Style has methods and techniques for operating in all of these ranges, though it prefers Medium/Close Range.

So, these are some of the important and vital concepts and "Kung Fu Roots" of the Shaolin Butterfly Style, and for most martial arts. In subsequent chapters we will now be examining the Shaolin Butterfly Style in great depth and detail.

Chapter Three: Exploring the Butterfly

Now that we have examined the lineage and various important concepts and general elements of the Shaolin Butterfly Style, let's begin looking at the style in more specific detail.

Butterfly Birth

All martial art styles and systems have an origin – a time and place when the art became distinct, was discovered, developed, or synthesized. Some are associated with a specific person or family, such as Bruce Lee and Jeet Kune Do, Gracie Ju Jitsu, or Yang Style Taiji. Other styles and systems are associated with a place – a village, city, temple or the like, such as Chen Taiji and the Chen Family Village, Shaolin styles and the Shaolin Temple, or Fujian White Crane/Fujian Province, China. Oftentimes these are blended; person and place were both important and influential in the development of an art. Such as Pai Lum of Dr. Daniel K. Pai and American Kempo of SGM Ed Parker, Sr., both born in the fertile martial arts culture of Hawaii, USA.

Dr. Daniel K. Pai, SGM Edmund Parker, GM George Dillman, getting ready to pick up Bruce Lee at the airport, early 1960's, photo courtesy of Mr. George Dillmanp

Sometimes the origins of an art are lost or shrouded by the mists of time, leaving us with only legends and speculation. The Shaolin Butterfly Style is one such style. Though we were given an origin story, the exact time and place and individual/founder are not known. Hopefully with more research and networking I can learn more, which is always a possibility as Chinese martial arts have been catalogued and systematized since ancient times.

I know a martial artist, tremendously knowledgeable and accomplished, who learned a rare Chinese style which had been preserved in Indonesia by the family of the famous teacher "Uncle Bill" de Thours; who he learned it from. On a trip to China some years ago he was in the park in Beijing practicing this style, and some old-timers were watching him intently, scratching their heads. After some time they went into a nearby building and returned, approaching this man with some books. The books had descriptions and pictures of the style he was practicing. The thing is, it had been extinct in mainland China since the 1600's! Somehow it had made its way to Indonesia and been preserved there. I can only hope that information like this exists out there somewhere regarding the Shaolin Butterfly Style.

At any rate, here is the origin story we were given. Long ago, no doubt in some exotic region of China, a Shaolin Adept was arrested and jailed, wrists tied behind his back. Being a Shaolin Kung Fu expert, strong and flexible (including mentally and spiritually) he decided to make the best use of his time as he could and practice his kung fu. So he squatted down to the floor and hopped over his bound wrists, thus getting his hands in front of himself.

Wrists still bound, he began exploring how this seemingly restricted position might work, kung-fu wise. Hour after hour, day after day he practiced and explored. When he was finally released, to his delight he had turned a negative into a positive, as he had discovered and developed the basis of a new, distinct style – the Shaolin Butterfly Style. To this day "bound wrist" techniques, forms, and applications are preserved in the style, honoring this discovery. Great thanks to this nameless Founder, as due to the sophisticated and advanced nature of the Butterfly technique it is comparable to the discovery of penicillin. Not planned but most definitely a valuable treasure which may benefit so many (kung fu wise).

Butterfly Infinity

Symbols are a natural and universal part of human culture, arts, business, and science. The letters and words you are reading, after all, are nothing more than symbols of human speech. From the "Golden Arches" to the Nike "Swoosh" the still mighty "$" to the infamous Nazi Swastika of the Third

Reich (a perversion of a revered, ancient spiritual symbol) – symbols are ubiquitous.

Here is an excellent definition of the word, taken from Wikipedia:

"A symbol is a mark, sign, or word that indicates, signifies, or is understood as representing an idea, object, or relationship. Symbols allow people to go beyond what is known or seen by creating linkages between otherwise very different concepts and experiences. All communication (and data processing) is achieved through the use of symbols. Symbols take the form of words, sounds, gestures, ideas or visual images and are used to convey other ideas and beliefs."

So, obviously symbols are also an integral aspect of martial arts practice, study, culture, and history – beyond merely as business marketing and branding tools.

As we have already discussed, and as the name explicitly suggests, the "Butterfly" is a key symbol of the Shaolin Butterfly Style, so much so that it is this beautiful creature that the style is named after. Elements important to the purpose of using "Butterfly" as a symbol for this style run from the physical and practical – the joined wrist methods, which look somewhat like a butterfly's wings – to the deeper and more esoteric aspects of beauty, transformation, and metamorphosis.

In addition to the "Butterfly" which is the outer symbol of the art, there is an "inner symbol" as well which is shared with initiates. This "inner symbol" has several variations and aspects to it, these being: the well-known "Infinity Symbol" the Ajna Chakra ("third eye"), the Om or Aum mantra, and the "Taiji-tu" symbol (often misnomered as the "yin and yang" symbol).

Let's explore these now, along with their relationship to the Shaolin Butterfly Style.

The "Infinity Symbol" is the most elementary of these "Inner Symbols" though this does not mean it is not profound.

It symbolizes the basic inner energy matrix of the style perfectly. Here is an excellent definition of the meaning of the "Infinity Symbol" taken from www.ancient-symbols.com:

"Originating from the Latin *infinitas* which means "unboundedness," infinity is the concept of endlessness or limitlessness most widely tackled in the fields of mathematics and physics."

In the context of the Shaolin Butterfly Style what this unboundedness, endlessness, and limitlessness refers to is the skill of being able to change and transform from one technique and style to another easily and seamlessly. This is a by-product of training well in this style and achieving skill with it. The internal energy constantly flows without interruption and never stops, she just changes and transforms.

Now, the "Infinity Symbol" also hints at Unity, which is represented by the point where the two ovals/circles intersect. In the context of the style this represents the unity of left and right, inner and outer, top and bottom, front and back, mind and body, technique and energy, and any similar dualities.

So, the "Infinity Symbol," represents going beyond duality to union and infinity. This leads us to our next aspect of the "Infinity Symbol" which is also a basic symbol of the Ajna Chakra or "third eye."

First of all, as stated the, "Infinity Symbol" is also one of the simple symbols which is sometimes utilized to depict the Ajna Chakra. A "chakra" is a center of power, of the universal life force, which exists in the human subtle energy body. "Chakra" means wheel (as in a vortex of energy) and they are often depicted as blooming flowers. Originating in ancient India, there are various Hindu, Buddhist, Sikh, Jain and other systems which make use of knowledge of the chakra's for health, vitality, creativity, spiritual growth, self-realization, and for other aims and objectives.

In the more well-known Indian yogic systems there are seven main chakras utilized, though various systems have identified and work with thousands.

These seven primary chakras are:

1. Root/Muladhara Chakra
2. Sacral/Swadistana Chakra
3. Solar Plexus/Manipura Chakra
4. Heart/Anahata Chakra
5. Throat/Vishuddah Chakra
6. Third Eye/Ajna Chakra
7. Crown/Sahasrara Chakra

The first five of these chakras are located in the central channel ("sushumna") with front and rear aspects; and they all are associated with various organs, glands, sounds, and colors. The chakra's do not exist in the physical universe, but interact with and influence it as two way transformers, receivers, and basins of energy. They perform many functions and are a fascinating study, but a full discussion is outside the scope of this work.

It is the sixth chakra, most well known as the "Ajna Chakra" that is associated with the Shaolin Butterfly Style. The Ajna Chakra is also known as the Third Eye, the seat of the soul, the brow chakra, the tisra til, the inner eye, the mind's eye, the sky eye, the tian-mu, and many other names. It is located between the eyes at about the brow level.

It is at the Ajna Chakra that the solar and lunar energy channels meet and duality is transcended, leading the student/yogi into Union. Qualities associated with an open and active Ajna Chakra include all higher aspects of mind, will, and emotion; intuition and imagination; higher knowledge, wisdom, and knowing. Along with self-realization, clairvoyance, gifted sight, and pre-cognition of varying levels. "Ajna" in Sanskrit (the ancient language of India) translates as, "command, perceive, and beyond wisdom."

So what the heck does this have to do with kung fu?

Keep in mind, the Shaolin Butterfly Style's lineage is Shaolin, which was the foremost Buddhist Temple in China since ancient times (not a commercial empire, as now). Thus, Shaolin arts and teachings have been influenced by Indian arts, especially the teachings of Lord Buddha and his disciples. Over time, naturally, indigenous Chinese Daoist, Confucian, and other teachings and knowledge intermixed with the "foreign" Buddhist teachings which began with Bodhidharma. This has resulted in the unique knowledge developed, preserved, and passed on via the many Shaolin teachings/systems. The martial arts systems were part of larger systems, containing teachings and methods on a wide range and variety of subjects. Being spiritual disciples, the goal was Buddhahood, for the sake of leading all others to this (in the classic Mahayana way known as "bodhicitta").

In modern times the Shaolin Five Form Fist system preserves this concept of teaching martial arts, in an interfaith form.

Specifically, the Ajna Chakra is associated with the Shaolin Butterfly Style as it is a High, Internal Style. A style in which when skill is achieved, duality is transcended and Union is achieved – as depicted by use of the Butterfly and Infinity Symbols. This isn't just in an esoteric or spiritual sense. A skilled Butterfly Stylist no longer has a left and right side, they have become totally unified into something new and unique. Similar to how a Butterfly's Wings must operate in perfect unison for flight to occur. We will be discussing this more in an upcoming section. Practicing and perfecting the Shaolin Butterfly Style aids in developing the Ajna Chakra as well. This is due to the nature of the techniques, which emphasize union of left/right, inner/outer, mind/body – leading to duality of mind/body being transcended.

The seed sound and mantra associated with the Ajna Chakra, and thus the Shaolin Butterfly Style, is the om or aum mantra. Om is the original creative vibration/sound of the Universe, known in the Christian Bible as "the Word." As it is written, "and God said, let there be Light." Om/Aum is this very sound, the sound of God. Mystics and self-realized Saints and yogi's can hear this sacred sound resounding in all. Utilizing ancient methods meditators may learn to follow this sound back to the Source (one such method being known as, "suratshabd yoga").

Another "Inner Symbol" associated with the Shaolin Butterfly Style is the "Taiji-tu" or as it is generally misnomered, "the yin and yang symbol." The Taiji-tu is ancient in China and utilized by many Chinese arts – cooking to martial arts.

First, a bit of background. As in various other topics we are introducing here, the knowledge and history of the "Taijitu" is very deep and beyond the scope of this work. But briefly, it is most important to understand that yin and yang do not exist alone, by themselves. There is only yin/yang, or more properly, Taiji. Discussing yin and yang (the elements of Taiji) serves only as a method to begin and further our understanding of Taiji. Yin/yang exists in endless pairs of relationships. Originally meaning the sunny side of the mountain (yang) and the shady side (yin). Depending upon season and time of day, the place and balance of sun and shade changes – which is one of the keys to understanding the Taiji-tu. So, yin/yang may symbolize male/female, hot/cold, day/night, left/right, shoe/foot, car/stoplight, and so many, many other such relationships.

What is yang in one inter-relationship may be yin in another, and vice-versa. The key is to understand the relationship of any pairs exists as its own reality, beyond the meaning of its component parts (a married couple is more than man and woman alone, for instance). Thus, it is a mistake to think of the Taiji-tu as a symbol of Duality – quite to the contrary. As with the Infinity Symbol, Ajna Chakra, and

Om – it symbolizes the Union of opposites and wholeness. It's just that they have not been completely transcended yet. Thus, Taiji-tu symbolizes the ideal Balance and Harmony to be found in our Universe and on Earth. To achieve this we must perceive ourselves in All, and All in ourselves. This is represented by the dots in the Taiji-tu, black dot in white "fish" and white dot in the black "fish." We must be flexible and non-resistant, open to both form and formlessness, change and flow in order to achieve this Balance and Harmony. This is represented in the Taiji-tu by the S shaped line within the circle. And we understand that all things – including ourselves – change and transform. This is represented as the ceaseless changing of yin into yang and yang into yin which the Taiji-tu depicts.

Transcending the Taiji-tu is symbolized by the empty circle, the symbol of Heaven or the non-dual realm, O. As we travel even further the circle itself dissolves and we enter the Buddha Realm. In martial arts there is the old teaching, "from large circles proceed to smaller circles; from smaller circles proceed to invisible circles."

This process of Taiji-tu to Empty Circle, Empty Circle to Dissolving the Circle (Invisible Circle) in the Indian arts is similar to the journey from Ajna Chakra to Sahasrara Chakra (crown), and from Crown Chakra to the Unbounded/Limitless, Mysterious and Eternal Realm (om tat savitur varenyam).

> Tai Chi is eternal. No boundary, no frontier.
> As tall as the sky. As deep as the earth.
> It may not be seen. It may not be touched.
> To seek the Tai Chi path is to see purity itself.
> May the Path be the guide,
> To the unfathomable depths.
>
> -Prof. Li Shixin

In technical terms of training and martial application the Shaolin Butterfly Style operates similarly to more well-known internal arts, such as Taiji Quan. It just has its own unique methods and methodology. We will describe and discuss this much more in later sections of this book.

To sum up, symbols associated with the Shaolin Butterfly Style include the Butterfly herself (the "outer symbol"), along with the "Inner Symbols" – the Infinity Symbol, Ajna Chakra, Om/Aum, and the Taiji-tu. Various combinations of these include:

Applications of these symbols run from concrete, practical training and martial application, all the way up to Personal Transformation and Self-Realization; all befitting a style as sophisticated and noble as the High/Internal Shaolin Butterfly Style.

The Butterflies Purpose

The purpose of the Shaolin Butterfly Style is two-fold. Both of which we have already discussed in general terms in the preceding section on the symbols of the Butterfly Style, and at other times. But specifically speaking, these two purposes are:

1. Training in the Shaolin Butterfly Style leads to a doubling of speed and efficiency of all known techniques. This happens if one trains well and for long enough. As we just discussed, the training leads to Unity – unity of left and right, mind and body, inner and outer, upper and lower, qi and technique, and more. Unity leads to Infinity. Unity and Infinity lead to

much greater speed and efficiency. The sophisticated nature of the training and the Butterfly techniques raises one's skill level all around.

I have had people I train with tell me it seems like I have four hands. My teacher has eight hands, it seems like anyway. Great thanks to him for sharing this special art with us.

Various martial systems each specialize in various skills, and training well in them will have definite results. For instance, both Bagua and Pekiti-Tirsia Kali promote excellent footwork and movement skills, each in their own way.

Judo, aikido, and shuai jiao practitioners who train well will have excellent throwing and falling skills, each in their own way. Many Korean and Northern Chinese martial arts are well-known for their kicking skills; just to give a few examples of how various arts are known to develop and feature certain skills/techniques.

2. Training in the Shaolin Butterfly Style leads to the ability to change and transform from one style or type of technique to another, easily and seamlessly. This, again, is due to the nature of the Butterfly techniques themselves as well as the Butterfly training methods. In fact, this is one of the reasons why the "Butterfly" is used as a symbol for the style. A butterfly starts out life as a moth; enters the cocoon; and emerges a beautiful, new creature – the butterfly. This journey of metamorphosis also symbolizes the journey of training in and attaining skill with the Butterfly Style. The Dragon in Chinese martial arts is also a symbol of change and transformation, along with other qualities, but with a unique perspective and approach.

So, training in the Shaolin Butterfly Style will enhance the ability to change from Striking to Grappling, Controlling to Takedown, Escaping to Countering, and so on. Additionally, the ability to change from one Animal or Elemental (Xing) to another is promoted – Tiger to Crane, Monkey to Dragon, Snake to Leopard, Thunder to Fire; and so on.

Butterfly as "Inner Connector Style"

It is due to these two purposes that the Shaolin Butterfly Style is known as the "Inner Connector Style" of the Shaolin Five Form Fist System; her "Mother System."

Shaolin Five Form Fist "Xing" Outline

Another configuration of style/class of technique which the Shaolin Butterfly Style also operates within as "Inner Connector Style" looks like this:

This was explained and illustrated to me in private moments with my teacher after a public seminar on the art that he taught. He diagrammed this and other info on the dry erase board, then held his hand open and used his finger-tips to name the 5 main Shaolin Animal Styles, and in the center of his palm he placed the Shaolin Butterfly Style (I added the Monkey to the diagram as it is also a key animal style in our system). This was an eye opening and highly educational moment, helping me to reach a new level of understanding of our system and the importance in the overall structure of the Shaolin Butterfly Style.

So, the Shaolin Butterfly Style binds all together, resulting in higher skills all around; such as doubling speed and efficiency and promoting the skills of Transformation and Change.

Other large, classic systems also have similar techniques (arts within them that are indispensable). For instance, Tuhon Bill McGrath of pekiti-tirsia kali always teaches that while the footwork methods of his art might make up only 5% of the total technique of the system, without them the art won't work combat-wise. My teacher taught me the same. While watching an arnis demonstration where the practitioner stood dead in place while performing snazzy stick techniques, he told me that no matter how skilled a Filipino stylist was with her weapons that without footwork he had nothing.

"Tui Shou" (push hands) inTaiji performs a similar function, being vital to developing the proper "touch" which then must be applied to self-defense applications and free-fighting ("san shou"). Tui Shou practice also raises the quality of one's empty hand Taiji art to a new level, as does the Taiji weapons practice. The mistake here with Taiji Tui Shou which is often made is to misunderstand it as Taiji self-defense applications or free-fighting, which it most definitely isn't. Tui Shou is a method of training for developing the proper "touch" as well as for practicing a variety of Taiji methods with a partner, and for developing and enhancing various other Taiji skills. To develop Taiji free-fighting skills one needs to be trained in how to bridge the gap from tui shou to san shou, and then to practice san shou and various san shou drills and training methods. A skilled, experienced instructor is needed for this. And yes, it is another topic for another day (and book).

Now, the Shaolin Butterfly Style can also serve as a "connector style" for practitioners of other systems as well. So if you practice armed and unarmed Japanese styles, training in the Shaolin Butterfly Style should only enhance your skills and aid in taking your style to a new level. I would say the same would go for any style or system which is compatible with a Chinese style, which is most. As the old saying puts it:

"All martial arts under heaven arose from Shaolin."

Butterfly Principles

So, we have already introduced, discussed, and explored many of the key principles of the Shaolin Butterfly Style. Here we shall list them, including some we have only hinted at or not discussed at all.

Butterfly Principles:

1. Union, Transformation, Infinity
2. Root, Stability, Mobility
3. Balance and Harmony
4. Form and Formlessness
5. Point and Circle
6. Transitional Techniques
7. Redirect and Act Previous

1. Union, Transformation, Infinity:

We have already explored these well, so here we shall merely list them as key principles.

2. Root, Stability, Mobility:

Being a Shaolin art building the root is one of the fundamental and key practices upon which stability is built and maintained at all times and in all situations. This stable root is then built into all applications of footwork and mobility, which is key to allow change and transformation to happen.

3. Balance and Harmony:

Although we have hinted at this, these are key aspects of the art which must be highlighted. Balance and Harmony are achieved via proper training over time. This includes both physical/technique wise; as well as spiritually, mentally, and emotionally. As we were taught, the most important time to practice kung fu is in the "kwoon of daily life." What we learn in our training is meant to help us with all of the challenges of life, as well as learning to be patient and enjoy each moment. Breathe in and feel the union with All. Breathe out and relax and find your center. All is well.

Respect, discipline, wisdom, and compassion are our most cherished treasures. Together they are the ingredients of Love.

4. Form and Formlessness:

Again, we have discussed these but due to their importance they must be listed here as key principles. "Form and Formlessness" describes the path of training from untrained novice to practitioner, practitioner to expert, expert back to the Formless Void. But they also describe tactics and techniques. Being an Internal Style the Form and Application of the Shaolin Butterfly Style depends upon the Formless Void. As an Internal Style, the Form and Application of the Shaolin Butterfly Style depends upon the Formless, Inner Form – this Butterfly has magic power! Yes, it can "float like a butterfly and sting like a bee" as well as become invisible, or appear behind you and clobber you over the head like double steel pipes.

5. Point and Circle

Again, hinted at, but as in all Chinese based systems, key concepts and principles. Here it is found in the "Infinity Symbol" – a point that joins two circles (ovals).

The Point technique-wise may represent the focal point of the transference of energy of any technique –be it a Ram's head punch or elbow Chin-na (locking/controlling technique).

The Circle represents the totality of the applications of any technique, movement(s), or posture. And of course, a circle contains infinite points.

The "Infinity Symbol" brilliantly illustrates the Point and Circle, along with other key aspects of the Shaolin Butterfly Style. Understanding of and skill with Point and Circle is one of the things which differentiates the true expert from the student/practitioner.

Transitional Techniques-
"Transitional Techniques" as the name suggests, lead one from another. For instance, parrying a punch, trapping the arm and pulling, then into a forearm – neck/head takedown, or escaping from a wrist grab and turning the tables into controlling the attacker's wrist.

As the "Infinity Symbol" suggests, the Shaolin Butterfly Style is essentially a system of transitional techniques and transformation of energy. "Transitional Techniques" is a concrete way of expressing and teaching this, which is emphasized right form the beginning with the first core "seed techniques."

Redirect and Act Previous-

Being an internal martial art, the Shaolin Butterfly Style is based upon these two key "inner skills" fundamental to many styles of "nei gong quan fa." The first level of internal skill is to, "absorb and redirect negative energy of word, thought, and deed." Being a true-life art and High Style, there is more to it than merely redirecting a punch. The inner negativities of bad habits and unbalanced emotions are much more danger-ous, insidious, and common, as are similar outer negativities which we may encounter in dealings with others.

So, "absorb and redirect negative energy" is just like it sounds – something has happened and we are dealing with it so it doesn't hurt us. As we gain in skill and especially experi-ence we move on to the next level of internal skills – "Acting Previous."

With "Acting Previous" we are neutralizing negativity before it can even manifest. This is a potentially very deep topic. Martial arts wise, quite simply "Acting Previous" may operate as avoiding dangerous places and areas; as well as being kind and respectful, humble and thankful. These go a long way in helping us to avoid all manner of trouble.

If an actual confrontation is unavoidable, say in a poten-tial physical altercation, "Acting Previous" will manifest as being able to sense the aggressor's intentions just before they manifest, allowing one to move and react in an optimal way to neutralize the threat. This is much easier said than done and requires expert instruction, daily discipline and practice (hours per day), and years of experience – "big kung fu!"

A batter in baseball only has tenths of a second to cor-rectly assess a pitcher's pitch – the very best major leaguers only get a hit 30% of the time. Of course, the fielders behind and around the pitcher also play a part in this low percent-age, but it illustrates the challenges of "Acting Previous" in a controlled situation.

In the often uncontrolled "battlefield of life" it can be even more challenging to always avoid trouble before it happens – perhaps impossible. But none-the-less it is a goal we strive for. One of the ways Dr. Pai taught my teacher about these vital concepts and practices was to teach seemingly contradictory concepts, leaving it up to him to reconcile them and find the truth. During self-defense training if my teacher anticipated at the wrong time, Dr. Pai would admonish him, "NEVER ANITICIPATE!" At other times when my teacher didn't antici- pate and was caught off gaurd Dr. Pai would admonish him with, "YOU MUST ALWAYS ANTICIPATE!' My teacher once gave me some great advice which I have never forgotten regard- ing achieving seemingly "impossible goals":

> "The key is to shut off the mind and perceive the world from the heart; then the Dao is a possibility and each moment is rich."

> -Tao Chi Li

So, these are some of the most important key principles of the Shaolin Butterfly Style. The list is potentially endless, but these will keep you busy for a while, so enjoy. In the following chapters we shall detail and describe the actual content and curriculum of the Shaolin Butterfly Style.

Chapter Four: Butterfly Foundational Methods

Introduction

So far we have been examining many of the general aspects of the Shaolin Butterfly Style, such as the lineage and various concepts and principles and related information, which is important in order to have a proper understanding of the style. Now we begin to discuss the actual techniques of the style: the foundational curriculum, the techniques, forms, applications and all else.

First of all, as we have discussed, the Shaolin Butterfly Style exists as a sub-style contained within a larger martial system; namely, the Shaolin Five Form Fist System. Students learning The Shaolin Butterfly Style traditionally began as students of this "Mother System" first, studying what is known as the "General Curriculum." Traditionally it was Sifu level instructors of this system who were taught the Shaolin Butterfly Style. Alternatively, it is possible that a Sifu level instructor of my teachers Taiji system or similar in his Kali Arts would have been able to receive training in the Shaolin Butterfly Style. To the best of my knowledge, perhaps only one or two individuals traveled that path to the Butterfly. I myself began training in my Teacher's Taiji system, then his Kali Arts and then his

Shaolin System. By the time I began learning the Butterfly Style I was a Sifu in his Taiji system and Full Instructor (Shr Shyung) in his both Shaolin and Kali Arts. Out of the many thousands of students my teacher had I was the only one who achieved this, eventually achieving Sifu level status in both his Shaolin System and Taiji System, as well as Full Instructor status in his Kali Arts. I was also Chief Instructor of the system for seven years, took over ownership of the school, training all students – including instructors—and am a lineage disciple of the art, my lineage name being Dao Chan I. Suffice to say I know the material well, and am proud and humbled to be a part in preserving and passing it on.

So, in this chapter I am going to introduce and describe the "General Curriculum" of the Shaolin Five Form Fist System, as essentially this has traditionally served as the foundation curriculum of the Shaolin Butterfly Style. In the following chapter we will examine the curriculum unique to The Shaolin Butterfly Style. At some future date, I hope to present a book or books detailing The Shaolin Five Form System and the "General Curriculum" in more depth.

One final note here—I am not making it a requirement that those interested in learning the Butterfly Style learn the entire Five Form Fist "General Curriculum" before I share the Butterfly Style with them. Whatever your background in martial arts, if you are a good-hearted and sincere person I am happy to share it with you. To paraphrase an old saying, "Have Butterfly, Will Travel"—or you can come to me.

General Curriculum

The Shaolin Five Form Fist "General Curriculum" is drawn from elements of the main sub-styles of the system – Northern Shaolin, Southern Shaolin, Quan Fa, Internal Styles, and Chinese Weapons. Chin-na/Grappling Arts are also included. All of the five main animal forms or Xing are here as well; Tiger, Leopard, Snake, Crane, and the Dragon. The purpose of the "General Curriculum" is to give students a well-rounded education in Chinese martial arts, practical and effective. From this "General Curriculum" a dedicated student may move on to focus on one of the specialty arts or curriculums, such as: Fujian White Crane, Shaolin Tiger, Wing Chun, Internal Styles, Chinese Weapons, or others.

This is a truly awesome system and I can personally attest to its effectiveness in multiple ways. No less an authority than famous Grandmaster, Dr. Maung Gyi, perhaps the world's leading authority on Asian martial arts, told me when I first met him that my teacher's system was one of the greatest martial systems in existence, feared even in China! This is quite a statement. Now, I am not looking to be feared, but this endorsement most definitely was appreciated and validated what we all knew. I thank my teacher for the great gift he shared with us, and know that the only proper way to thank him is to continue on developing myself as he taught us to, and to continue to share the art with others. This book is part of that process. May the blessings be.

Now, at one time the Shaolin Five Form Fist System was one of the official curriculums of the Kuoshu Federation, R.O.C. In fact, I have a curriculum manual (a tome, really) from 1980 detailing the "General Curriculum." My teacher's version is slightly different, reflecting his own unique experiences and insights. Being a Headmaster of the system it is perfectly within his rights to do this. In fact, in my time with him (17 years full-time) he adjusted the "General Curriculum" several times; always seeking to improve it. Change is, of course, one of the key principles and concepts of the arts, and of life. A martial system which does not evolve and adapt as needed, is a dead system. This is very much a dynamic, living one.

Let us now examine the elements of the Shaolin Five Form Fist System "General Curriculum." The "General Curriculum" again being essentially the foundation curriculum of the Shaolin Butterfly Style.

Basic Training

This is the all-important foundation level of the art, and encompasses all manner of foundational exercises and methods which build basic skills, strength, flexibility, endurance, coordination, power, breathing and qi, and more. There is too much material to list and describe, so I will merely highlight some of the key methods.

Traditionally, in Chinese martial arts, this material is known as Ji Ben Gong. Ji Ben Gong is described by the well-known teacher Bruce Francis on his www.energyarts.com website as "Ji Ben Gong: the basic power training through which all Chinese martial arts develop the type of power they specialize in." To see a wonderful, in-depth presentation of a traditional Ji Ben Gong Style I recommend people read the great book by Dan Miller and Tim Cartmell, Xing Yi Nei Gong: Xing Yi Health Maintenance and Internal Strength Development. At some point, I plan on writing a series of books on the Shaolin Five Form Fist System, building on what I am presenting in this book. This will, of course, include a complete presentation of the basic/Ji Ben Gong of the system's "General Curriculum." Each of the sub-systems has its own specific Ji Ben Gong as well.

Another way to view this basic training Ji Ben Gong is to compare it to military basic training. It not only gets you in shape, it prepares you for all that is to follow in subsequent training and for "real world" application.

Here is a listing and brief description of some of the key methods utilized to train students in the Shaolin Five Form Fist System. Remember, as taught by my teacher and how I learned, this is also part of the foundational level curriculum of the Shaolin Butterfly Style.

Break Stance and Ceremonial Bow

The Break Stance and Ceremonial Bow are the first two methods the student learns, and are in fact the seeds which contain within them the entire art. As such they are vital methods, and how seriously and sincerely one practices them will determine the quality of everything else one does as a student.

The "Break Stance" is also known as the "Kung Fu Salute." In the various lineages and styles of Chinese/Asian martial arts there are numerous versions of this vital method. Within the Shaolin Five Form Fist System, in fact, there are several variations utilized, besides the standard one pictured here. Each variation has its own meaning. The "Break Stance" is what is known in Indian arts as a "mudra." A "mudra" is a symbolic posture, gesture, or movement(s). It represents a kind of physical/psychic code language. Mudra is in fact one of the natural acts of human life and culture. For instance, as in waving the hand "hello," or nodding ones head in agreement—yes!

The basic Kung Fu Salute is made by standing straight with the feet together. The right fist is placed against the left open palm at upper chest height, forming a triangular type shape with the hands/arms. The elbows are down and shoulders as well, with the fist/palm brought together in the center of the chest. When utilized to begin or end a training session the eyes look straight ahead to the horizon. If the Kung Fu Salute is utilized to pay respect to a Sifu or class-mate or the like, then one looks at them and performs the gesture.

The closed right fist symbolizes "power" and the open left palm "control." When they are brought together as in the Kung Fu Salute it naturally means "control over power." This is the basic meaning in our lineage. Thus it has the added meanings of balance and wisdom, as well as compassion as it is a gesture of Respect. It may also symbolize the union of Yin and Yang (Taiji), hard and soft, internal and external.

In the context of formal training it is utilized to begin and end a class, to ask a question, pay respect, say thank you, and in other ways. The teacher will also utilize it in the context of training in order to focus students and teach them to be in the moment, by hitting the drum and yelling "Break!" during key moments of training. At which times students will snap to attention in Break Stance and shout "Shr!" Shr is a (Chinese) positive affirmation, like shouting Yes! I am awake! I am here! Yes!

Again, these are some of the ways that we were taught to utilize the Break Stance. Other styles and lineages will have their own methods. The importance of this vital method cannot be overstated. We were taught that this seemingly simple gesture contained within it, in a seed form, the Entire Art. Food for thought, which I have chewed on well for thirty years now, and cannot disagree with. Funny but illustrative story: about twenty years into my training I knew that the art had settled into my heart, and that I was totally kung fu crazy, when I awoke one night around 3:00 A.M. with the intense need to heed the call of nature. Groggily, I made my way to the toilet and flipped up the seat—then totally naturally and with no forethought—I stood bolt upright and gave the toilet my very best Headmaster Kung Fu Salute! Damn, I shook my head once I realized what I had done, and proceeded to let Nature flow. Later I pondered the meaning of it all. Obviously the toilet is a most important item in the household, deserving of respect for the service it generally unfailingly gives. In that moment, needing to relieve myself urgently, that respect and appreciation manifested itself in me spontaneously offering the toilet my best kung fu salute! I was actually quite proud of this—my teachers' efforts were not in vain!

Similarly, a student of mine once stopped to pick-up Chinese food at a restaurant near where she lived after class one night. This particular night she neglected to change and went in to pick up the food in her traditional Assistant Taiji Instructor's Uniform. When the people brought out her food she was so appreciative that she unconsciously gave them her best Taiji Salute and Bow—and they gave her the food no charge! Such was her sincerity that the owners of the restaurant were deeply touched and appreciative of her heartfelt gesture.

Now, the Ceremonial Bow is also a mudra, but in this case in the form of a set of movements. Typically, one performs the Break Stance and then follows with the Ceremonial Bow to begin and end a class. The Ceremonial Bow is what is known as a "Salutation Ritual." It performs several important functions all at once. Technique wise, along with the Break Stance, it is the students' introduction to Kung Fu/Taiji movement and technique. It is like a simple form/kuen/kata, complete with its own self-defense applications. Spiritually and mentally it is a method of learning to focus and polish one's will, attention, heart, and sincerity. By sincerely performing the Ceremonial Bow, from the heart, we both ennoble and humble ourselves; thus opening ourselves to the Higher Self and Higher Powers. So this seemingly simple and perhaps superfluous ritual in fact holds great power. It is, in fact, one of the "secrets" of Kung Fu/Taiji training, so practice it well and sincerely.

Stances, Stance Work, Breathing

This includes not only learning all of the foundational stances, but also various methods of stepping into the stances as well as stepping and moving through the stances. This level is like a baby learning to walk. It may not be pretty and it may hurt, but it is absolutely necessary. Quite simply, no stance + no breath = no Kung Fu!

Some of the methods include; Stepping to a Stance, Stomping to a Stance, Circle Step to a Stance, Sink to a Stance, Hop/Jump to a Stance, and more. These are also combined with various arm motions and breathing methods, including Kiai/martial sounds. Kiai (Qi-he in Chinese) is itself a key practice and study, one which we are not going to explore very much for now, as it is very specialized.

Briefly, Kiai is a Japanese word composed of two parts: Ki (qi) – The Life-force/breath and, "ai" or Harmony. We are using this Japanese term in the context of a Chinese martial system as it is such a ubiquitous, well known and excellent term. With Kiai we are bringing into harmony our technique, our life force, and the life force of the universe. Depending on the technique and Kiai utilized there are differing specialized applications and effects.

The two basic Kiai of the Shaolin Five Form Fist System are the Tiger Shout and the Snake Breath. There are actually two versions of the Snake Breath at this basic level, dynamic tension Snake Breathing which builds inner strength and power; and the Snake Shout. The Snake Shout isn't really a shout at all; rather it is a very focused internal breathing method coordinated with various strikes and techniques, utilizing the snake sound, sssssssk!!

The student is also taught another specialized Kiai known as the Spirit Shout (or, White Dragon Spirit Shout, Pai Lung Qi He). The Spirit Shout is a special Chinese Kiai which aides the student in developing fighting energy. This fighting energy is a force/power which comes from the earth and flows upwards and outwards through the student. The Spirit Shout is in fact one of the secrets of the Shaolin Five Form Fist System. Every living creature/animal is endowed with this protective fighting energy. Even a meek little mouse, when cornered can be dangerous. Mastery of the Spirit Shout takes the student and his technique to an entirely new level. Practice well.

So again, these and other breathing methods are combined with learning the stances and stepping methods. Basic stances include: Break Stance, Ready Stance, Horse Stance, Bow and Arrow Stance, Cat Stance, Cross Stance, Crane Stance, Spinning Top Stance, and False (Heel) Stance. There are many others, but these are emphasized at the novice level and serve as the foundation for all else. Again, the hands and breath/sound are incorporated in a variety of ways such as the Five Step Horse Stance, which includes specific hand and foot motions combined with the breath to learn to make a Horse Stance. It also has fighting applications, as do all of these methods.

Stretching Methods/Leg Exercises

Here we have all manner of floor stretches, splits, leg lifts, joint rotations, and specialized exercises – such as the Chinese leg exercise, the spider stretch, and the circling palm. There are also standing stretches, partner stretching methods, yoga asanas, and leg and arm swinging methods. All of these exercises are taught as formal drills which include the use of the hands and feet combined with the breath. Such as Stomping to a Bow Stance and giving a Spirit Shout while simultaneously shooting out a Spear Hand and doing a series of front leg lifts.

The key is to build whole body flexibility, suppleness and healthy, functional joints. The legs, hips and spine are very important to develop due to their importance in health and longevity and delivering power in martial applications.

Strength/Power Building Methods

These include vital methods such as snake push-ups, the stomach connection exercise, a.k.a. iron bridge, the muscle grouping exercise, Grandmaster's exercise, slow squats, one-legged squats, frog leaps, duck walking, spider walking, and many others. The goal here is to build strength and power which is functional for a traditional combat style Chinese martial arts system, and which also promotes health and longevity. So these methods differ somewhat from traditional sports/fitness style methods which focus on building muscles primarily, and in isolation (such as standard weight training). The traditional Kung Fu strength/power developmental methods are generally whole body methods which also incorporate the use of the breath and work from the inside out. Bodhidharma's teaching of the "Muscle/Sinew Change" are woven into all.

As an example, we can highlight the Snake Push Up. You spread your legs about double shoulder width apart and place your palms on the floor, from a standing position. Walk your hands forward a bit. Begin the forward Snake Push Up by lowering the side of the face to the floor, then the chest, abdomen, and hips as you slowly shift your weight forward towards and through your hands. As you shift forward, your hips scrape across the floor, and using your shoulders, you lift your chin up to the sky, stretching and arching your back into a yoga-like pose. Now, shift your weight backward, lifting your hips, back to the starting position. The starting position looks something like the Yoga asana known as Downward-Facing Dog. After doing a series of forward Snake Push-Ups one precedes to reverse/ backwards Snake Push-ups. Here the process is reversed – lower the hips as you lift the chin, and slide backward to the starting position.

These exercises stretch and strengthen the whole body, with an emphasis on the spine and shoulders. In Chinese martial arts the spine, hips, and shoulders are vital areas for issuing force from the ground upward and outward so they must be strong and supple. This makes the Snake Push-Up an absolutely essential Kung Fu power method, more so than the standard Push-Up.

There are, as mentioned, many other similar methods such as: Tiger and Leopard Push-Ups, other Snake exercises, and more.

Other Stuff

Other basic training methods include things like jumping jacks of all kinds; running in place, climbing the mountain, jog around the kwoon/block, dragon walking, and more. Basic training also includes drilling on basic striking and blocking methods and body conditioning/tempering methods like iron palm and the like. Being more specialized I am going to present them under their own heading.

Conditioning /Tempering Methods

Body conditioning and tempering is featured right from the beginning in the Shaolin Five Form Fist "General Curriculum," and the serves as a key foundation for the Shaolin Butterfly Style. Proper conditioning, such as soft iron palm/cotton palm training is vital for the safe and effective use of the Shaolin Butterfly techniques. This was a point emphasized by Grandmaster Clarence Cooper in various conversations we had about the Shaolin Butterfly Style. GM Cooper was a close student of Dr. Daniel K. Pai for years, and one of the top full-contact fighters of his generation. In fact, no less an authority than famous Grandmaster, Dr. Maung Gyi told me that GM Cooper at one point back in the 1970s was the top full-contact fighter – bar none – worldwide. His reputation as a devastating fighter is well known in Pai Lum circles. GM Cooper told me that he made great, effective use of the Butterfly techniques in these hard-core matches.

He emphasized that proper conditioning was key to the use of the Butterfly techniques, both in the ring and on the street; otherwise one would injure oneself. My teacher also felt the same, witnessed by the importance he placed upon body and hand conditioning in our system...and internal stylists out there, this goes for you too. One can't fight unless one is conditioned to be able to safely give and receive contact. No ifs, ands, or buts.

Body conditioning/tempering methods can be utilized on the whole body, except for the throat. Best to avoid the genitals as well, though very specialized methods were developed for this sensitive area. There are few teachers who know these methods, and possibly less who would like to practice them now, so we will just say – like the throat, no tempering of the genitals! You'll just end up hurting yourself.

Basic methods include conditioning the forearms and shins with various partnered "body pounding" methods, such as performing closed fist 3 and 5 Star Blocking Patterns with a partner. These methods, and all body conditioning methods, need to be learned from a skilled and experienced instructor, live and in person. There is much more to it than just smashing yourself until you are black and blue. Done properly, your bones will gradually get thicker and harder without injuring yourself. Done improperly, you may face nerve damage, disease, and even death. It isn't a macho game, but rather an art and skill which has been developed over centuries.

In addition to conditioning methods done with a partner, such as Kicking/Punching and Blocking Drills, there is equipment which may be utilized for when there is no partner available. One of my favorites is the wall-mounted ironwood mook jong or wooden dummy, which can be utilized to practice all manner of techniques upon and results in most effective conditioning of the body and of our "natural weapons." There are many, many other training tools as well – from wall-mounted punching boards, to wooden forearm/shin conditioners and more.

Students of the "General Curriculum" are also taught how to utilize the iron palm bag and develop the, "soft iron palm/hand." This is also known by some as the Cotton Palm. Properly done, one's hand gets thicker and softer while circulation of blood and energy is enhanced. Simultaneously, the bones of the hand and fingers get thicker and harder.

There are similar methods, as mentioned, for conditioning the entire body; resulting in something called the "iron body." Some of these methods are quite sophisticated. As a whole these methods are known as, "Iron Skills."

A key part of these Iron Skills is the use of internal and external herbal medicines and liniments. My teacher had numerous recipes for these special herbal blends, known as "dit da jow". There are jows/liniments for use before training, post training, healing, bone bruises, and on and on. There are also internal herbal pills which one can take in order to aid healing while training and developing Iron Skills. I highly recommended Sifu Dale Dugas in this area as he personally makes his own herbal concoctions, which are of high-quality. He has decades of experience and is an expert in the martial arts with advanced Iron Skills. He is both a great guy and a true gentle giant who happens to be badass, super knowledgeable and skilled. Check him out at www.daledugas.com

My instructor is not only advanced in Iron Skills, but also in very rare, high-level palm and fist internal methods – such as vibration palm and suction palm. All of his skeleton/bones are 10 times thicker than the average human male, as x-rayed by his perplexed chiropractor who just scratched his head when he got the x-rays and said, "whats with your bones?" Trying to strike him is like striking the Gorn from Star Trek. Good luck – dinosaur bones strike back -ouch! After being hit, beaten on, knocked down, etc...by him for 17 years straight, there aren't too many people out there that I have a hard time with. Of course, I am not looking to test myself vs. Andre the Giant or Shaq – not without a 10 gauge shotgun, cocked and loaded anyway.

Supplementing the conditioning/tempering methods and adding balance and safety are various methods of health promoting Qi Gong and Nei Gong, including Muscle/Sinew Change methods and forms. Health and longevity are the first and final goals of the art, which must never be abandoned.

Qi Gong/Nei Gong

As we discussed in Chapter 1, Shaolin teachings encompass three broad categories which together form the Shaolin Way: Shaolin Kung Fu, Shaolin Qi Gong, and Shaolin Chan.

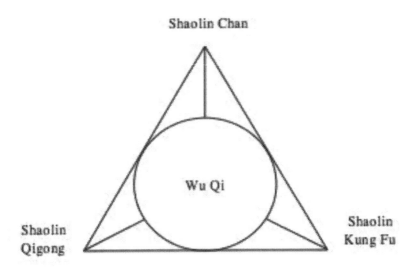

The Three Treasures of Shaolin

Properly taught these elements of Shaolin overlap and inter-penetrate each other – they are not separate. Thus, practicing a Shaolin form such as the Butterfly Energy Form or Taming Tiger or the like, is both Kung Fu Martial Arts and Qi Gong. It may also be viewed and practiced as meditation in motion, and as such, part of Shaolin Chan practice, especially as one gains familiarity and skill with a form.

However, it is useful as well to approach them as distinct disciplines in order to promote the unique characteristics, applications, and goals they each contain. This book is focused on presenting a unique Shaolin Martial Style, the internal Shaolin Butterfly Style. So the main focus of the book is on the Shaolin Kung Fu aspect of the art. But just as we briefly examined Shaolin Chan due to its importance, we shall now examine Shaolin Qi Gong in more depth.

The Shaolin Five Form Fist system contains many, many variations and methods of Qi Gong and Nei Gong. Qi Gong refers to exercises which circulate energy whilst utilizing bodily movements – either stationary or with steps: standing, seated, or lying down. Breathing and breath development is also key to Qi Gong. My teacher generally referred to it as "Health Nourishing Exercise." Meaning, utilizing Qi Gong to nourish our health at all levels of being. This is a practical definition of Qi Gong, not a straight translation from Chinese to English. It is a simple but excellent definition for it captures the essence of what Qi Gong is for – utilizing Qi Gong methods to nourish health and promote regeneration, maintenance and longevity for Spirit, Mind, and Body. Concepts such as balance and harmony are also key to good Qi Gong practice.

There is also Martial Qi Gong, which the Shaolin Five Form Fist System also preserves and emphasizes; and Spiritual Qi Gong such as the methods of Shaolin Chan. These three being the main types of Qi Gong: Health/Healing, Martial and Spiritual Qi Gong. Traditionally in China there were various "schools" of Qi Gong and each had its own unique and distinctive history, curricula, methods, goals and intentions. The schools were:

- Daoist School
- Buddhist School
- Confucian/Scholar School
- Healing Qi Gong (medical) School

Health/healing Qi Gong is often referred to as "Medical Qi Gong" but I prefer to avoid using this term as in the West medicine is generally thought of as something taken to fix what is broken or unbalanced. Qi Gong is ideally utilized to avoid illness and imbalance, and maintain harmony and promote longevity. Qi Gong is in line with the old saying "an ounce of prevention is better than a pound of cure."

Shaolin Five Form Fist was, obviously, originally born of the Chinese Buddhist Qi Gong/Martial/Spiritual Tradition. However, being an American alive in the year 2018 and given the art is a living art, any and all appropriate methods may be utilized and incorporated into the system – given they are in harmony with the original root foundation of the art. The tradition I come from is well-known not only for its practicality and traditional methods and philosophies, but also for its innovativeness and creativity. This is one of our lineage's strengths, and I have continued on in this fashion, as I was taught.

Soon after beginning with my training in Taiji I learned the Transcendental Meditation technique (T.M.) of the great Maharishi Mahesh Yogi; and began studying the works of ParamahansaYogananda and many, many others since then. In fact, since childhood I have been interested in learning about Eastern traditions, philosophies, and martial arts. One of the very first books I read as a child was <u>The Prophet</u> by Kahlil Gibran which I found to be pure magical literature (my Mom had a copy and I first read this book around age five).

Along the way, over the past 30 years, I have been blessed to receive training, initiation, empowerments, darshan, satsang, shaktipat, and taken refuge with and from, numerous world-renowned meditation and spiritual teachers. Compassionate leaders such as: Dr. Maung Gyi, Gen Sherab Kelsang, Mirabai Devi, Shri Anandi Ma, and Sant Rajinder Singh . All of this and more – such as training with numerous experts of martial arts, Taiji, Reiki, Yoga and the like – coalesces into my understanding of Shaolin Five Form Fist and the Shaolin Butterfly Style.

Students of Shaolin Five Form Fist begin learning Qi Gong as part of their martial studies and practice, as the concepts and practices of Bodhidharma's Muscle/Sinew Change are integrated into learning the curriculum. There are also specialized sets which teach this, such as the Monks Dawn Meditation Form (a.k.a. Monks Tension Form). Students are also introduced to various simple but powerful Shaolin breathing methods, such as Cloud Breathing (Upper and Lower Cloud Breath) and dan-tien breathing methods; as well as Yoga asanas which assist with relaxation and proper breathing (Corpse Pose and Crocodile Pose). There are many classic Shaolin Health Qi Gong methods as well, such as: Embrace Heaven and Earth, the Phoenix Spreads His Wings, and Bend the Bow and Shoot the Arrow, amongst others.

There are standing and seated meditation methods, such as the standing Lotus Palm Meditation and Triangle Meditation, Silent Sitting, Contemplation and Mantra Meditation.

Nei Gong Refers to "inner powers" or "inner skills." The main difference from Qi Gong is that these methods do not involve any bodily motion. It is a pure internal art, coordinating spirit, will, and qi. The basic Nei Gong method is the Embrace the Tree Posture (single and double weighted). This may be practiced in a variety of ways, from simple standing and breathing to various internal energy methods (like "Gold Light Nei Gong"). Other methods of Nei Gong include "Circular Breathing" and the "Internal Pyramid" Nei Gong among many others.

Both Qi Gong and Nei Gong may involve inner visualization of color, shapes and geometry; as well as breath and sound. They may also utilize internal pathways of energy. My teacher's foundation teaching is very similar to what GM Bruce Frantzis has presented in his wonderful books, such as the classic Opening the Energy Gates of the Body. This is a Yin or as Mr. Frantzis describes it "Water Method." It is a very safe and powerful method which focuses on releasing, letting go of, and dissolving blockages of energy. We were also taught what Mr. Frantzis refers to as "Fire Methods."

To properly describe all this would take more than one book. Also, as in all good Chinese systems, Qi Gong and Nei Gong are embedded into the learning and practice of the entire art. Famous "Living Treasure" GM Fu Shu Yun emphasized this on one of her visits o our school, saying quite simply, "Taiji IS Qi Gong." The Shaolin Butterfly Style adds its own unique methods, which as previously mentioned focus on unity, transformation, and infinity.

One of the keys of Qi Gong practice and martial arts as well is known as the "Three Harmonies." These are often referred to as "The Three Regulations", but I believe the word harmony conveys a more balanced meaning. They are:

- Harmony of the Mind/Will
- Harmony of the Breath/Qi
- Harmony of the Body

Each one of these areas needs to be harmonized individually, as well as in concert with the others. There is a simple formula often utilized to convey the "Three Harmonies" – Yi – Qi – Li, which are Chinese words referring to the will/intention aspect of the mind; Qi or Life-Force, which is intimately in tune with our breath; and the body and physical aspect, or Li.

As to how exactly this is done, one must seek out a qualified Instructor. It involves properly coordinating and utilizing our mind and awareness, breath and body – as in posture, alignment, stance, tension/relaxation, and the like. Proper practice engenders a state of consciousness known as the "Qi Gong State" which is something like the Relaxation Response and Meditation in Motion; a most wonderful place to be, indeed.

The following principles are also key to proper Qi Gong practice, especially to allow the spiritual dimension to flower:

- All is One, We are One, One is All
- Everything is Energy
- Spirit Commands Energy
- Thy Will be Done, not mine (drop the small self, embrace the Larger Self)

Falling and Rolling Methods

Falling and rolling properly are skills which are vital to every martial system. Of course, there is quite a wide variety of application and practice here. There are arts which spend much of their time on the mat – such as Judo and BJJ, and those which avoid it such as Kickboxing and Kali (for good reason.) Regardless, as I say, having even rudimentary falling and rolling skills is a must – yes for you too Taiji players. When one has no fear of falling one's balance and sense of rootedness is enhanced greatly.

Now, as both the Shaolin Five Form Fist System and Shaolin Butterfly Style are traditional Chinese combat systems – not designed for sport – they take a very practical and measured approach to this vital area of training and practice. Namely, while falling and rolling skills are indeed essential, the ideal is to train to keep one's balance and not fall. Falling and Rolling skills are primarily back-ups and fail-safes, not primary strategies or basic tactics. Unlike in the ring, street type encounters run the risk of having multiple attacker scenarios manifest and being on the ground is a definite liability in those circumstances as it would be on a battlefield.

If one does happen to get knocked down or fall during a confrontation the sooner one gets back on one's feet the better; which is part of the skills learned in falling and rolling practice. Of course, there are specialized ground fighting methods; in the Shaolin Five Form Fist System the Snake, Leopard, and Spider Styles all have unique ground fighting applications.

Tuhon Bill McGrath, one of the leaders and pioneers of the Pekiti-Tirsia Kali System here and worldwide, was a court officer in New York City for many years. He told us of the many, many cases he personally knew of where two guys would get into a scuffle, start to grapple and hit the ground and continue to scuffle on the ground. Whereupon one of the combatant's girlfriends would stab his opponent while down! Or his friends would pitch in breaking bottles or chairs on his opponent while down. So, while it is true many confrontations go to the ground, that doesn't have to be and shouldn't be the end – learn how to make the ground your friend and fall and get up like the old Rock'em Sock'em robots – don't stay down.

Fighting on the ground is very specialized and is a worthy and ancient art. There are Chinese and Tibetan snake boxing arts, for instance, which go back centuries. In modern times MMA and BJJ are very popular. Whether ancient or modern, however, fighting on the ground is a specialization, according to the view and understanding of traditional combat martial arts. Learn to keep your balance and unbalance your opponent instead. If you do fall, get right back up! We would practice hitting the ground and getting up constantly, as the Sifu beat the drum and shouted commands. Keeping one's balance is also part of what the emphasis on stance in Chinese Arts is about. This, in fact, is part of the key, bedrock first level – which must never be lost or sacrificed.

The very first kick defense I learned in Shaolin Five Form Fist involved standing in a Bow and Arrow Stance with my arms held behind my back while the tough-as-nails Sifu delivered flying side-kicks off my abdomen. The idea here is not just to toughen one up but to learn how to use breath and stance properly in order to receive the force without being hurt or unbalanced. The next level is learning to return that force.

Now, there are also more subtle benefits to developing falling and rolling skills. When one no longer fears falling, balance and confidence on one's feet moves to a higher level. Like learning to swim makes boat travel more enjoyable. I would even recommend introducing falling and rolling to elder Tai Chi students (appropriately) for just this reason, as well as general body conditioning.

Technically speaking the foundation methods of the Shaolin Five Form Fist Shaolin system and Butterfly Style are the following:

- Hitting the ground and getting up quickly from a standing, walking, or running position
- Front Break Fall
- Side Break Fall
- Rear Brake Fall
- Forward Roll
- Backward Roll
- Chinese Roll

Initially these methods are taught in a very controlled way, broken down into steps and taught step by step. They are not acrobatic, but meant to be functional, basic skills. Over time and with practice they can evolve into more challenging and unpredictable methods. One way my teacher trained us was to have us do a running, jumping/flying forward roll over a staff that he held. While we dove over the staff like Superman he would strike sharply upwards, hitting us to test and challenge us. Many similar methods were employed in our training in order to perfect stance and balance.

The Shaolin Five Form Fist System also preserves various animal-based ground fighting methods such as those of the Leopard, Snake and Spider.

Blocking/Deflecting Methods

Blocking and deflecting are vital to martial arts training and combat. There are a wide range of techniques and styles – from the hardest forearm blocks to feathery soft palm deflections. Regardless, the number one rule for blocking is this – never block unless you have to! If attacked one wants to counter in a decisive way to end the encounter. Blocking is primarily passive and is to be avoided, although with time and training even palm deflections can become bone-breaking and punishing.

The Shaolin Butterfly style is very specialized and features numerous joined wrist/palm/hand techniques and methods, including specialized blocking and deflecting techniques. The methods learned in the Shaolin Five Form Fist "General Curriculum" lay the foundation for those specialized Butterfly Style methods.

First off, some definitions: "Blocking" refers to harder, more right angle methods of countering an opponent's attacks – such as closed fist forearm blocks utilized against an attacking punch, kick, or grab. They can become very powerful. Proper blocking – even the powerful kind – never utilizes a dead, sledge hammer – like type of energy, however. As in many other types of technique, one learns to move from a place of relaxation to a place of momentary tension/ focus (the block), then right back to being in a relaxed state. Blocks must remain springy and alive. This allows for change and adaptability to be preserved so that the flow of combat and being in the moment isn't broken. This must be learned from someone live and in-person, and is just one of a million reasons why martial arts can't be properly taught and transmitted via video/internet.

In addition to blocking, there are deflecting, parrying, and passing methods. These are generally performed utilizing the palm and are much softer and internal in style, allowing for more efficient and subtle counter-attacks.

The basic method taught in the Shaolin Five Form Fist System is a fantastic method known as "5 Star/5 Sector Blocking" and it contains both blocking and deflecting methods and can be performed numerous ways: Open Hand, Closed Fist, Single 5 Star, and Double Hand 5 Star. The 5 Star/5 Sector is in fact almost like its own system of training and it is quite deep.

"Star" refers to the points of the pattern, which represent points of contact (blocks/deflections). Like a five pointed star:

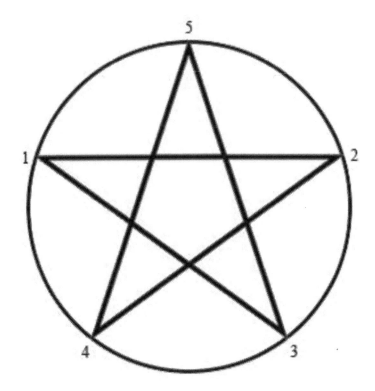

"Sector" refers to the space between the points/blocks such as between one and two or three and five. Star and Sector give us two ways to practice and view the same method. For years my teacher referred to it as star, emphasizing the points. At a certain point (no pun intended), he changed and emphasized the sectors, or spaces, which leads to a more fluid understanding of the technique.

The foundation 5 Star/5 Sector method is the single hand 5 Star/Sector Drill. From the 5 Star fighting position one performs the following right handed -

#1 – Palm Deflection
#2 – Back of Wrist Deflection
#3 – Lower Palm-Heel Deflection
#4 – Lower Palm Deflection
#5 – Rising Dragon Tail Block

The "Dragon's Tail" in this instance refers to a specialized way of utilizing the forearm to block or deflect. The Dragon Tail technique in general can be compared to how an alligator uses his tail to knock over prey. As humans we of course do not have a tail, but we do have arms and legs which can both be utilized in Dragon Tail fashion. As far as the arms are concerned the fleshy top and bottom portion of the forearms is used for Dragon Tail type technique, such as the #5 deflection in the 5 Star/Sector Blocking Pattern. When the bones of your inner and outer edges of the forearms are utilized then the technique becomes what is known as "Dragon Wings."

Thus, the 5 Star/Sector drill also serves as an introduction to Dragon Style technique. The 5 Star/Sector Drill can also be done with a closed fist, in which case each block becomes a closed-fist forearm block.

The 5 Star Sector Drill can also be performed with both hands at once, the Double 5 Star/Sector Drill. Here each hand moves through the 5 Points; just two different points simultaneously.

Double Five Star/Sector Pattern

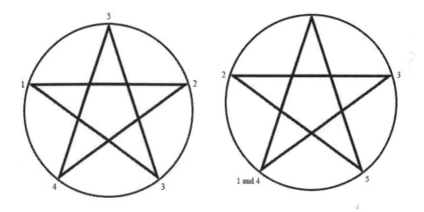

Of course, The Double 5 Star/Sector drill can be performed with the left handed leading, in which case the above-described patterns are reversed.

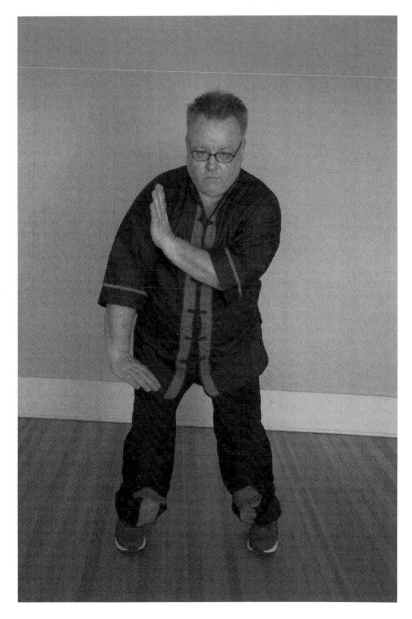

Other foundational blocking/defecting methods contained within the Five Form Fist Shaolin "General Curriculum" include the inner and outer circle blocks. A circle, of course, contains infinite points. In the case of the 5 Star/Sector Drill, 5 Points on the circle, which are important to learning proper blocking/deflecting skills, are emphasized.

With the circle blocks one learns methods which rely upon the entire circle. Each hand learns to trace either an inward or outward flowing circle, utilizing whole body movement. Initially they are performed from either a Horse Stance or a Ready Stance. They are very similar to the Chen Style Taiji "Silk-Reeling Drills."

Both the 5 Star/Sector and Circle Blocking Drills have a multitude of ways of being practiced. This includes solo and partner drills, as well as upon apparatus (such as the mook jong), and a variety of breathing methods.

They lay the foundation for all other blocking/deflecting methods contained within the Shaolin Five Form Fist System as a whole. Various methods include:

- 3 Star
- 5 Star
- 7 Star
- 9 Star
- Circle Blocks
- Crane's Wings
- Butterfly Blocks, Deflections, Wings
- Dragon Tail Blocks
- Many others

Apparatus/Training Equipment

Working with training equipment and training apparatus is a vital practice for all martial arts students and practitioners, Butterfly Stylists included. While there have been some fantastic and sophisticated training tools developed over the centuries (the legendary Shaolin Hall of Dummies comes to mind), with creativity even ordinary objects can be utilized to great effect. Magazines, rolled up newspapers, wiffle ball bats, pillows, duct tape, rope and the like can all be utilized to safely enhance training.

Training equipment and apparatus are utilized in order to develop and enhance vital Kung Fu skills and attributes, such as: speed, focus, timing, power, conditioning, and coordination. Even if one is blessed with many training partners they can add a unique and indispensable dimension to training.

Initially, students of the Five Form Fist "General Curriculum" are introduced to specific equipment that is needed to match development of the skills and techniques they are learning. These include:

- The air shield
- Focus pads
- Focus mitts
- Heavy hanging bags
- Double-end bags
- Wall boards
- Forearm/Shin conditioner
- Heavy medicine bag
- Mats
- Jump rope
- Iron Palm bags

As a student enters intermediate-level they are introduced to and instructed in the use of the wall-mounted ironwood mook jong (wooden dummy). This is an ingenious training device which can be utilized in a wide variety of ways. This includes diverse skills such as Taiji sensitivity drills, multiple blocking and striking sequences, pushing and pulling methods, and more. The mook jong is famously utilized to great effect in the Wing Chun style – it is often called The Wing Chun Dummy, but any style can benefit from practice on the mook – Dragon, Crane, Butterfly, Taiji, Wing Chun, Kali – you name it!

Training on the mook jong not only builds and enhances skill; it also conditions the body parts utilized for safe "real world" application. As in Iron Skills, the use of a good dit da jow is recommended.

There are quite a few versions of the mook jong, actually. The advantages of the wall mounted dummy are that it can be struck and kicked full power, and it has a springiness to it that gives a more realistic, live feeling to the practice. One needs to learn how to utilize and properly strike the iron-wood mook jong (or any mook) from an expert as improper use can cause injury (including serious, irreversible nerve damage).

This has always been my favorite piece of training equipment, which I worked on regularly for many years in a variety of ways. One was to strike the solid body of the mook (ironwood) 100x daily (as often as I could) with a downward, flowing palm strike – full power and full range of motion. It made such a loud "smack" sound that it rang throughout the entire school, raising eyebrows. My teacher loved it! A visiting Sifu from Hong Kong who had attended the same Wing Chun Club as Bruce Lee admired my mook skills, remarking that I was lucky that it is ironwood or otherwise I would have broken the mook to bits striking it.

At any rate, these are some of the basic tools utilized as training apparatus in the "General Curriculum." There are many other methods as well, including utilizing the weapons themselves in various ways (jumping over saber slashes, dodging spear thrusts, and the like), kicking dixie cups off a partner's head, and many other ingenious ways of developing skill. The Butterfly Style specializes in using rope, including tying the wrists together. There are entire forms done this way.

One of my Kung Fu Brothers specialized in Fujian White Crane Style. Our teacher tutored him in building a wooden lattice-like structure (which was hung from the ceiling) and from it hung numerous striking bags of various sizes. He would stand under the latticework (square with criss-crossed pieces of wood interlocked) with bags hanging around him like planets of various sizes and practice White Crane footwork and striking methods. He would target striking the bags while moving in all directions. Similar ingenious training methods exist for all specialized skills- Phoenix Eye to Snake's Tongue; ward-off arm to spinning top.

Striking Methods

To review, here in Chapter 4 we are introducing and briefly discussing the foundation curriculum of the Shaolin Butterfly Style. This foundational curriculum is known as the Five Form Fist Shaolin "General Curriculum." There is no way in this simple introduction to properly describe all of the various methods, exercises, drills, and applications contained within the "General Curriculum." To do so would take several volumes and multiple videos.

At any rate, striking is of course a key and famous aspect of martial arts in general, and of our lineage in particular. Dr. Daniel K Pai's striking power and skills were demonstrated publicly and privately many, many times – leaving those who witnessed his feats awestruck. The famous Grandmaster Dr. Maung Gyi referred to Dr. Pai as the "Chairman of the Board" and the "best ever to come from the United States" regarding striking and breaking skills. High praise, and well deserved.

The Five Form Fist Shaolin "General Curriculum" contains a plethora of striking methods. Here we will only list the foundational methods:

- Vertical Front Punch
- Horizontal Punch
- Hook Punch
- Backfist
- Spear Hand
- Knife Hand

- Ridge Hand
- Tiger Claw
- Dragon Claw
- Hammer Fist
- Single Headed Dragon Punch
- Phoenix Eye Punch
- Leopard Fist Strike
- Ridge Palm Strike
- Elbow Strikes
- Knee Strikes
- Front Thrusting Heel Kick
- Side Thrusting Kick
- Rear Thrust Kick
- Snap Kick
- Roundhouse Kick
- Inner and Outer Crescent Kicks
- Flying Crescent Kick (Tornado Kick)
- Stomp Kick
- Toe In/Out Kicks
- Spear Kicks

Note that with many of these striking methods there are a variety of ways to perform them, depending on the range, style and various other factors. Each method is learned and practiced a variety of ways:

- By the count, broken down into steps
- With speed and power
- Various breathing methods
- Solo
- Partner
- vs. equipment/bags, apparatus
- Application with a partner
- Slow, medium, full speed and contact sparring

Multiple Techniques/Articulation Drills

As the title of this sub-section suggests, these are drills where multiples of techniques are performed in order to perfect the ability to flow from one technique to another. Along with the flow of the multiple techniques, focus is on developing the speed, power, and precision of each individual technique. Hand and Leg Articulation Drills and Multiple Technique Drills are vital to take one's skill to higher levels.

Potentially, any series of techniques put together by a competent Sifu will work, such as Vertical Front Punch, Outer Circle Block and Front Kick Combination. The more skilled and experienced a student is the more challenging the combinations may be. An advanced student might practice a combination of techniques such as a Flying Crescent Kick, a Spinning Top Sweep, and a Back Heel Kick Combination switching legs with each technique.

In addition to combinations which a Sifu will devise for each student in the "General Curriculum," there are several formal exercises which are taught and emphasized, including the following:

The Spear, Ridge, Chop Combination Drill

This drill utilizes both hands to deliver double Spear Hand Strikes, followed up by Double Inward Short-Range Ridge Hand Strikes, immediately followed by Double Outward Short-Range Knife Hand/Chop Strikes.

Initially this drill is taught, like all basics, in a formal fashion following the commands of the Sifu and the beat of the drum. Dynamic Tension Breathing and focused Snake Breathing will be utilized, along with natural breathing. The drill performs multiple vital functions all at once, such as learning to coordinate mind, breath, chi and techniques all from the stance/root and dan-tien. This enhances and builds the student's precision, power, and control. A variety of stances may be utilized, including: Ready Stance, Horse Stance, and Bow and Arrow Stance.

Essentially this is a Double Hand Crane technique (Southern Style), so the drill also serves as an introduction to that style of technique and energy. Performing the drill with both hands at once requires greater focus and connection to the root/stance and dan-tien. Of course, the drill can be broken down and practiced single-handed later as well with movement/steps, and with a partner including adapted to self defense and sparring.

Punch-Grab-Block Combination Drill

This drill introduces not only the performance of multiple hand techniques, but also changing from closed to open hand techniques. It is performed one hand at a time.

Initially this drill is performed from a low, wide Horse Stance utilizing the 5-step Horse Stance method. Again, as with all basics, it is taught meticulously and in a variety of ways and breathing methods. The hand techniques are as follows:

- Either a Vertical Front Punch or a Horizontal Punch
- An Inner or Outer Circle Palm which flows into a Tiger Mouth grab, pulling the elbow into chamber against the ribs.
- Followed by a Lower Palm Heel Block performed on a slight downward angle from right to left (with the right hand)
- This is then followed up by a Rising Right Armed Dragon Tail Block

One then performs the sequence with the left hand. The initial punch is done with a Tiger Shout, each successive technique with the snake kiai (ssssk!) – unless it is being practiced with Dynamic Tension Snake Breathing.

Dragon Claw-Rake Drill

This is another double hand articulation drill, which combines striking with clawing/pulling/raking utilizing the Dragon Claw. This drill is performed initially from a low, wide Horse Stance utilizing the 5-step Horse Stance Method, and chambering both hands at the ribs. From here, the student performs a Double Ridge-Palm Strike followed up simultaneously by a Double Downward Pulling Dragon Claw Raking Technique. A "Ridge-Palm Strike" is a special Open Palm striking technique which utilizes the upper fleshy portion of the palm just below the base of the fingers. The hand is slightly tensed and formed into a shape which accentuates the Ridge-Palm. Striking with the Ridge-Palm say to the forehead or collarbone, delivers a stunning, destabilizing type of blow which lends itself to being followed up by Claw/Grabbing Techniques (hair grab, claw the face, pull the opponent inward).

Again, a variety of breathing methods are utilized in teaching and learning this awesome drill and technique.

Chinese Leg Exercise

This is a challenging leg exercise where one stands on one leg with the hands in the 5 Star Guard Position and works the other leg through a variety of kicking positions and foot formations, holding each one for a count of 10 or more. I forget which movie it was in, but I distinctly remember seeing the Little Dragon himself, Bruce Lee, working through this great exercise with much power, control and grace.

There are a number of possibilities/positions possible, the following routine being typical:

- Stand in a Crane Stance (single leg) with hands in 5 Star Guard
- Extend the raised leg, pointing the toe waist-height – hold for a count of 10

- Next, the leg stays there but adjust the foot posture to the Ball of the Foot position – hold for another ten count
- Without lowering the foot, now change the foot position to a knife edge of the foot position – hold for a count of 10
- Now without lowering the leg, pull the foot inward to make a Lifting Crane Stance – hold for a count of 10
- Next extend the leg sideways into a Side Knife-Edge Kick position – hold for a count of 10
- Return to the starting position and repeat

This is obviously an extremely challenging drill; a beginning student may need to utilize a chair back or the like to hold to assist them in maintaining balance. An advanced practitioner will perform with the leg/foot positions held at head height. Other positions are possible as well, including kicking formations to the rear. Good luck!

Sweeps, Takedowns, Throws

These categories of technique all involve knocking the opponent off his feet and to the ground in a variety of ways.

Before they can be learned one should be proficient with Falling and Rolling Methods, which are vital fundamentals. Ideally, *one never wants to take a fall in a combat situation*! Rather, we train to learn to stay rooted and to be able to successfully counter any sweeps/takedowns/throws which are attempted upon us. But of course, we must prepare for the worst. As discussed, learning Falling and Rolling Methods are also vital just for its own sake, to build confidence, suppleness, and health.

Let's now discuss what makes a Sweep a Sweep, a Takedown a Takedown, and a Throw a Throw:

Sweeps

A sweep is a very powerful method of potentially unbalancing and violently knocking an opponent to the ground. Done well they can be devastating, unpredictable and difficult to defend against. There are Standing Foot Sweeps and Squatting/ Spinning Sweeps.

When one performs a sweep the sweeping foot stays very close to the ground. One may use the Inside Edge, Outside Edge, Heel, or Bottom of the foot to sharply strike and dislodge the opponent's foot. The hands and whole body are utilized to facilitate the sweep (for the standing sweep).

The ideal time to sweep the opponent's foot is just as he is transferring weight to it, but has not yet rooted the foot.

Essentially, there is the Inside Sweep and the Outside Sweep (inside or outside of the opponent's foot). When one falls from receiving a sweep done well it can be devastating, uncontrolled, and the ground is very unforgiving. The best sweep and take down has the sweeping foot staying close to the ground and the body stays upright. Unlike in sport styles where one may bend over at the waist and lift the sweeping leg high in the air, in a combat system one is ever mindful of maintaining balance as there is no referee on the street or in the battlefield.

Now, in the Five Form Fist "General Curriculum" there are also the Low Squatting and Spinning Sweeps known as the Spinning Top and Iron Broom. These methods are performed from the low Squatting Stance known as the Spinning Top Stance.

-Spinning Top Stance:
One squats on the ball of one foot, lifting the heel. The other leg is extended out sideways with the foot held flat on the ground in a special foot shape which is a variation of the knife-edge foot position. The leg is held rigid like a baseball bat from hip to foot, and one spins a full 360° circle when performing the Iron Broom or Spinning Top Sweep.

-Iron Broom Sweep:

One spins forward and strikes the opponent's ankle/foot with the inside portion of one's ankle.

-Spinning Top Sweep:

This is reversed, one spins backward striking the opponent's foot/ankle with the heel of the extended, sweeping foot.

These are very challenging techniques to master. In fact, I have yet to see one performed properly on TV or in a movie; they are always done sloppily and with bad, weak form. There is quite a bit of solo and partner training which goes into developing these techniques – including just being able to squat on one foot, extend one leg, and form the stance properly. I remember – ouch!!

When mastered and performed with good timing these are both devastating techniques. One wants to perform the Spinning Top or Iron Broom when the opponent is vulnerable and unable to counter attack. One strategy utilized is to aim the sweep toward the rear leg of the opponent, as targeting only the front leg may make it too easy for them to evade the sweep.

I will never forget coming to class one day as a new student and noticing that the floor of the main Kwoon had what to me looked like crop circles worn into the finish of the wood floor. Upon inquiring about this strange looking scene it turns out that the Headmaster had been drilling the Instructor Class in the Iron Broom/Spinning Top Sweeps the night before. So much so, that they had worn circles into the wood! God bless our teacher who always taught us with such patience and discipline, expecting us to strive for perfection – always.

Takedowns

As we were taught, a Takedown is distinguished from a Sweep or Throw in that you are primarily taking the opponent down utilizing one's own hips/legs in a maneuver that is sometimes called a "Leg Trip". Only one of the opponent's legs leaves the ground on a Takedown; whereas with a throw, both of his legs come off the ground. Essentially, there is an Inside Takedown and an Outside Takedown, depending on whether the Takedown is performed on the inside or outside of the opponent's leg/hip. Use of the hands and especially the hips is key in performing a successful Takedown.

Although the basics of both Sweeps and Takedowns are seemingly simple, there are endless variations due to the variety of set-up and finishing techniques available. For instance, the "Dragon Wing Takedown" is a devastating technique, one which requires superb timing and skill to perform properly. The "Dragon Wing" refers to the inner and outer edges of the forearms – the bony parts – which are utilized to violently strike the neck while simultaneously one's raised leg Sweeps/Strikes the opponent's leg, knocking him to the ground mercilessly. There is also a "flying" version of this technique, which is very fast and powerful, utilizing the "High Moon" technique but no sweep.

With the Hidden Foot Maneuver one learns that virtually any series of techniques can have a Takedown added to it.

Throws

As mentioned, what distinguishes a Throw from a Sweep or Takedown – as we were taught – is during a Throw both of the opponent's legs will leave the ground as he falls. Although we were taught a number of Throws and the concept of the Throw in general, our teacher did not emphasize them. In our system, Sweeps and Takedowns are emphasized, as they are better integrated into our overall system of attack and defense and better fit the combat nature of our art.

There is a saying in Chinese martial arts, "every step is a kick and every kick is a step." By Kick and Step, one may infer more broadly "Leg Maneuvers." This includes Sweeps and

Takedowns. This is one of the key inner secrets of Stances and Stance Work, combined with Stepping Methods and Kicking. Thus, even a simple Horse Stance contains unlimited applications – train hard and train well!

Application/Self Defense Sets

As an integrated, traditional Chinese martial arts system, virtually every aspect of learning Shaolin Five Form Fist is connected to self defense and combat, one way or another. Every exercise, every drill, every form, the rituals utilized, the code of conduct, the ceremonial bow – everything relates directly or indirectly to learning and perfecting the, "Art of Destruction," as Dr. Maung Gyi referred to it to me.

A full discussion of this is beyond the scope of this simple introduction. Quite simply, to the uninitiated, the Break Stance and Ceremonial Bow are methods of demonstrating respect and sincerity; and of developing character and confidence. To those who know, while this is true, there is more – they are also self-defense methods with many applications.

So, learning self-defense and the combat aspects of the system – including the Butterfly Style – is a never-ending journey for the disciplined and creative student. There is always more to uncover and to learn and relearn. My teacher describes the art as a never-ending buried treasure – the more you dig, the more there is. I have been digging for 30 years now and I understand this in a way I couldn't when I first heard it. Yet there is still so far to go, so much to learn – and unlearn. As the old teaching puts it-

- *In the beginning, as a novice, uninitiated student, a punch was just a punch, a kick just a kick.*
- *After training for some time and gaining some real basic skills and knowledge, I definitely knew that in fact, a punch WAS NOT just a punch; a kick NOT JUST a kick – they were so much more!*

> - *As I continued on for many more years, developing my art and myself, I came full circle back to the beginning. A punch was just a punch, a kick was just a kick! No big deal.*

So, all of the training methods, all of the concepts and principles – all of it is designed so that with enough practice and time the art becomes natural – not contrived, not foreign or separate from oneself, not theoretical or technical. It is as natural as breathing and one's heartbeat. As my teacher loved to say: "Boxing (Chinese martial arts) is like taking a walk and throwing a punch like snapping your fingers." It should be that easy!

Leaving the philosophy aside for now, technically speaking applications and self-defense are learned initially by learning the basic uses and applications of the techniques one is learning. There are many drills and methods for each and every technique taught. There is much too much of this to get into here in this simple overview, but briefly some of the methods include:

- Practicing a single technique versus a single technique, such as Vertical Front Punch versus a number #1 Palm Deflection
- Practicing multiple techniques versus multiple techniques – 5 Hand Strikes to different zones/targets versus the 5 Star/5 Sector Blocking pattern
- Practicing applications at varying speeds and tempos: slow, medium, full speed and power, broken tempo, slow/rhythm (change speeds)
- Practicing applications in place utilizing various stances
- Practicing applications while moving, such as "One Step" and "Three Step" sparring
- Preset application practice and freestyle application practice
- Utilizing various breathing methods
- Practicing at different ranges – close, medium, long range

- And many other practice methods

Now, in addition to learning the uses and applications of the basic techniques there is learning the basic applications of the movements in the forms. Forms Training is very deep and we will explore them in their own subsection next. Initially the focus is on learning and performing them well with accuracy, speed and power and all of the important elements required. Along the way, formally and informally, the student begins to learn the purpose for the steps, motions, twists and turns of each and every form. As this begins to happen ones concept and understanding of the art—as well as one's "toolbox of techniques"—takes a quantum leap beyond the basics. Again, we will discuss this more in the next section. Each and every form contains unique methods, applications, energies, strategies and tactics and in our system has been chosen very carefully to complement each other and serve as a foundation for further training and growth.

Another very important part of learning the art of self-defense in our system is the learning and teaching of formal self-defense sets. Sets contain all manner and style of attack/defense combinations. Strikes, Kicks, Grips, Claws, Takedowns, Chokes, on and on. They allow the student to begin to learn more complex combinations of attack/defense/controls/escapes; slowly at first, building up to full combat speed and power. The self defenses are organized into sets which each focus on a style and class of techniques such as "Hidden Foot Maneuvers" "Arts of the Temple" "Purifying the Garment," and the like. The system these sets come from is a traditional Quan Fa system preserved by the Kuoshu Federation, R.O.C. known as "Chinese/Hawaiian Kempo."

Kempo (or Kenpo) is a Japanese way of saying " Ch'uan Fa/ Quan Fa" or "Arts of the Fist." The fist is a symbol for martial arts in general which has the underlying symbology of the "Hidden Fist" or the "Fist within the Fist."

Chinese/Hawaiian Kempo? I hear some of you thinking. Yes, indeed. In fact, over the centuries the Chinese – and their culture and arts – have traveled and been transplanted everywhere, including the Aloha State. So, there is also Chinese/Filipino Kung Fu, Chinese/Malaysian Kung Fu, Chinese/Indonesian Kung Fu, and so on. In this case Chinese/Hawaiian Kempo is an old, traditional version of what influenced many other American Karate Styles – such as the American Kenpo of the famous SGM Ed Parker. Interestingly enough, Dr. Daniel K. Pai and SGM Edmund Parker were cousins, as related to my teacher by Dr. Pai and confirmed to him by none other than SGM Parker himself (at a book signing where he met him.)

In many Pai Lum lineages Chinese/Hawaiian Kempo is known as "White Lotus Kempo." At any rate, regardless of what one calls it, it is a tremendous martial system in its own right. Unlike most Chinese systems it is taught primarily via the basics and self-defense sets – hundreds of them. There is only one form, an internal flowing Monkey Set which is designed to balance the energies of the self-defense sets.

In our system there is also preserved, something which is known as "Chinese/Okinawan Kempo" which is best exemplified by the Pai Lum form "Chinese Soft Fist, " a tremendous set of Chinese and Okinawan style techniques seamlessly woven into one beautiful form (more on that in the next section.)

In our system, our teacher emphasized the pure Chinese style as well as the Chinese/Hawaiian style over the Chinese/Okinawan style. However, he did share with me that he felt that the best styles overall, in his estimation, were the Chinese (including Chinese/Hawaiian) and Okinawan styles (such as Goju and Uechi.) As for weapon styles he very much appreciated and respected the Filipino Styles, but I digress.

Lastly, in the course of learning applications, self-defense, and combat students are taught various Martial Concepts and Principles, and how to apply them. At a deeper level are the Martial Energies and Elementals. These include Concepts, Principles, Elements, Animals, and Energies, such as:

- Angle, Range, Zone
- 3 heights of stance and their purpose/use
- 3 Gates—Upper, Middle, and Lower—otherwise known as the Head of the Dragon, the Body of the Dragon, and the Tail of the Dragon
- Body Mechanics and their applications
- Energy Power Flow Dynamics such as: reeling silk and pulling silk
- Animal Xing: Dragon, Leopard, Tiger, Snake, Crane, Butterfly, Deer and the like
- Elementals: Earth, Water, Metal, Fire, Space/Ether/Void, Lightning, Wind and the like
- Much more

So, as you can see learning applications, self-defense, and combat in Shaolin Five Form Fist is a very deep art. It is also very practical, having been developed via a high-quality lineage and the synthesis of the best teachings of many famous and legendary teachers. Much gratitude and respect go to my teacher and his teachers and all the teachers of the lineage for their parts in learning, developing, and passing on this great art. It is a humbling honor to be a small part of it.

Forms Training

As we have discussed and diagramed The Shaolin Butterfly Style is the "inner connector style" of its Mother System, the Shaolin Five Form Fist System. It has its own unique methods, techniques and forms; it exists within and as a part of this larger system. There are many similar examples of systems like this—Xing-Yi and Bagua Systems with their multiple interconnected animal and elemental styles, Pekiti-Tirsia Kali with its long, medium, and close range weapons styles and unarmed styles, and so on.

Given that the Shaolin Butterfly Style and Butterfly Styles in general are so rare, I wanted to be thorough in presenting the art both on its own, and as part of the larger system to which it belongs.

To reemphasize, traditionally the Shaolin Butterfly Style was primarily taught to Sifu level instructors who had learned the Shaolin Five Form Fist "General Curriculum" and had graduated on to more specialized studies. In this section, we continue briefly describing and introducing this "General Curriculum," moving on to the forms.

Although they have been key elements in Chinese systems for centuries, in the past when the martial arts were closer to their roots as methods of combat and self-defense Forms Training was not as emphasized as it is today. In the past, Forms Training was one element of an integrated system of training, secondary in the grand scheme of things compared to mastering the basics and applications, conditioning for combat, and developing "Kung"- Martial Power (of one sort or another).

Having said this, let me make clear that I am not disparaging Forms Training—on the contrary they were and are vital to comprehensive martial arts training, as well as preserving and passing on the various unique and distinct styles which have been developed. Traditional Forms Training serves many purposes, such as:

- The traditional forms are a repository or encyclopedia, which contain the accumulated knowledge of martial arts combat of the experts with decades of experience distilled into movement sequences
- As such they contain techniques, tactics and strategies obvious and hidden, waiting for the disciplined and dedicated student to uncover

- There are different types of sets or forms which have differing intents – some are martial forms and some are geared more toward exercise or fitness, some very specialized – such as focusing on muscle/sinew change or another important aspect of the arts
- There are empty hand forms, two person combat forms, even multiple person combat forms, weapons forms, show forms, beginner, intermediate, and advanced forms, and more

Additionally, Forms Training is a great way to develop attributes, such as:

- Balance and coordination
- Changes in speed, tempo, and rhythm
- Deeper breathing, endurance, and breathing methods
- Concentration, relaxation, meditation in motion
- Power/ Energy Flow Matrix—at a deeper level each form contains its own Energy Flow Matrix, this is the level of the essence, Xing (shapes/form) and spirit of the form

Forms can be very simple to extremely challenging and advanced. Traditional methods include practicing atop polls which are placed in a pit with spears embedded into the bottom of the pit – don't slip! In our system there is a form known as the "Thousand Steps." "Thousand Steps" is a Northern Shaolin style set, preserved in our lineage and various Pai Lum lineages. What not all know, however, is that performance of the "Thousand Steps" actually entails much more than this form alone. To practice the "Thousand Steps" entails practicing each and every set in the Northern Shaolin Curriculum, one after the other; which is then capped off by performing the form which is named "Thousand Steps." I only know one talented and dedicated individual who even came close to performing this achievement, so challenging it is. Learning all these sets properly takes years, to say nothing of the physical conditioning needed to do this.

Speaking of "performance" traditionally one does not perform a form the way they do it today due to the influence of modern Sport Wushu. You are not putting on a performance for an audience to be judged, like a "Kung Fu's Got Talent" television show! One practices the forms and performs them to achieve skill and accuracy, each according to the requirements of the various styles the forms come from. It isn't a performance art! "Performance art" Kung Fu is just that – a show. It isn't the real thing, like "Gunsmoke" isn't really what the American Old West was all about (sorry partner!) – I have nothing against modern Sport Wushu, mind you, we just need to be clear in our understanding and teaching.

Regarding Forms Training, there are quite a few ways they can and should be practiced, such as:

- Slow speed (like Taiji,) medium, and full speed and power
- Practice with different breathing methods, depending on the requirements of the style
- Practice the form by the count, step-by-step, one move at a time holding each posture – alternatively every single movement can be broken down into sub movements
- Practice the form by sections, such as five or six moves, pause and repeat – do this with each section of the form
- Practice the form left handed in all the same ways as you do right handed
- Practice outdoors in various environments – grass, dirt, mud, sand, beach, in the surf or water, wind, rain, snow, as many different ways like this as you safely can – dedicated and advanced experts have been known even to practice on the roof of a building during a hurricane! I did something similar once on the beach in Southern Maine – quite a challenge – the winds blew me all over but I never fell

- Many other ways to practice, such as legs only, upper body only, under a table – be creative and go for it!

Now, as for mastering a form, this takes a minimum of three years of daily training in a focused and disciplined way (see the preceding discussion and more) including learning the obvious and hidden applications of the form. So truly, in Forms Training one should never be bored, there is always more to learn, and unlearn.

Again, virtually all styles of Asian martial arts make use of forms training – some more, some less. A few of the names for what in English we usually call a form or set are:

- Taolu – Mandarin Chinese, sequence of martial arts movements
- Kuen- Cantonese, a set of movements, also means fist method,similar to QuanFa
- Kata – Japanese term for a set of martial arts movements (and others), probably the most recognizable term here in the USA.
- Hyung/Poomse – Korean terms for forms
- Yudham- Sanskrit term for combat sets
- Dui Da – Mandarin Chinese for a 2-person combat form
- Many, many similar terms

Now, there is quite a bit more we could say about Forms Training in general, but this shall suffice for this brief overview and introduction. Let's move on to the basic sets (Kuen/Taolu) of the Shaolin Five Form Fist System.

First off, contained within the various sub-systems of this system are numerous, perhaps hundreds, of sets. I honestly don't know, but even just the ones I have knowledge of runs into dozens. My teacher has a photographic memory for martial arts. Combined with a most unusual talent and discipline and wide and deep training – from here, to Canada, Hawaii,

Hong Kong, Taiwan, Japan, and Okinawa. Everything he has learned fits into the System, one way or another.

The forms of the "General Curriculum" lay the foundation and introduce the basics for all of the major subsystems and more.

Sub-Systems of Shaolin Five Form Fist

Major Animal Sub-Styles of Shaolin Five Form Fist

There are 11 main forms in the "General Curriculum" as I learned it. Each form has a focus and a purpose in relation to learning and mastering this great system.

1. The Three Short Forms of the Tiger

These are three short sets (often grouped together) of Shaolin Tiger Technique. Tiger Is the foundation technique and energy of many Chinese styles – yes, it's even in Taiji! The three short forms of the tiger are: Short Form of the Tiger, Movements of the Tiger, and Twist of the Tiger. FYI, there are no proper videos (like on YouTube,) out there that I have seen of these simple but excellent, essential forms; just some very poor quality versions.

2. Lau Ch'uan Shu

Lau Ch'uan Shu is a set of static postures of primarily animal postures (some elements) from the famous Lau family system – it is also known in English as "Animal Sequence Movements." This is true, old-time Kung Fu –the opposite of flash—you form a stance/posture and hold it 10 seconds to five minutes or longer for each posture of the set.

3. The Monk's Tension Form

A key Shaolin internal/external set, this is also known as the "Monk's Dawn Meditation Set." This is a form which makes use of dan-tien centered Tension Snake Breathing, based upon Damo's teachings of "Muscle/Sinew Change."

4. Elbow Sequence

This is a flowing set of primarily elbow techniques of all kinds. This is not the set utilized in many Pai Lum lineages; at a certain point my teacher left that one out, replacing it with this more fluid set.

5. Chinese Soft Fist

This is the first full-length form taught in the curriculum. Chinese Soft Fist is what is known as a "Bridge Form" – it is composed of a blend of typical Southern Shaolin Chinese-Style techniques/movements, and those of a more typical Okinawan Style/origin. Thus whether one is moving from a harder style to a softer (more Chinese Style) or from a softer to a harder (more Okinawan Style) this form facilitates the transition. Regardless, this is an absolutely outstanding set preserved within the PaiLum lineages as well as here in the Five Form Fist Shaolin System. The set is also known as "Leopard Fist" due to the many Leopard Style techniques and movements it contains.

6. Lau Gar

This is a famous set again from the Lau family tradition which is utilized in many Hung Gar traditions and here as well. However, our version is much more flowing than the versions I have seen online. Indeed, this is the great virtue of the set – constant flowing combat energy, as exemplified by its Energy Flow Matrix and multitude of all manner of effective techniques – high to low, close to long range. This set also exemplifies an atypical style known as "Southern Longfist."

7. Taming Tiger

This is the famous set from the Hung Gar traditions. My teacher learned three versions of this tremendous and challenging set – a traditional Hung Gar version, a Black Tiger version, and the PaiLum version. Dr. Pai was a martial arts genius with a huge, deep knowledge base. As he learned traditional sets, he would add his own particular touch to each. He, of course, also created forms and styles. At any rate, the version we were taught was the Pai Lum version which is a very obvious version of the famous set of Hung origin. It contains a large variety of excellent hand and leg techniques, footwork and breathing methods.

8. Liang Jen Ta (Combat Form)

This is a traditional two-person set typical of Southern Shaolin Styles. One practitioner/side is focused on Tiger Style Technique, the other on Crane. The energy and the tempo of the form build to a crescendo. Combat or two person forms aid in further developing timing, control and various other key factors.

9. Ling Po Ch'uan (Lian Bu Quan)

This is the first set of Northern Shaolin Style techniques and curriculum which is taught. This is a very famous and widely dispersed set; it was utilized as part of the basic training of Chinese troops in World War II, and by many military and police academies today. In English the name means "Consecutive Steps Fist/Set," or is often referred to as "Linking/Continuous Steps." It contains numerous highly practical self defense techniques and teaches many important fundamental basics. It appears to be originally from a Northern, perhaps Tibetan, Crane origin.

In our system is also preserved an Internal Arts version of this set, as a part of our Internal Arts curriculum. It is an excellent complement to standard style Tai Chi movement, as it moves in a primarily linear (North-South) sequence.

10. Monkey Stick

Monkey Stick Is the foundational Staff set taught, and is a short set full of excellent and important fundamental Staff techniques. It is a flowing and mobile set which is from a Southern Crane Style originally.

11. Fu Mei Don Dau

This is the famous Southern Shaolin set known as the "Tiger Tail Knife" set, utilized in numerous Southern Shaolin systems. It powerfully combines the energies and techniques of the Tiger and the Chinese broadsword/sabre into one tremendous set. Very practical techniques, beautiful to view, fun to practice. Great stuff!

So these are the foundation sets of the "General Curriculum." Although there isn't a Jian/Gim set taught in the pre First Higher-Level curriculum, sets of Jian/Gim basics and applications are. The forms come later.

Again, there are many, many other sets in this system. Some of the more well-known and best/most important ones are:

- Outer Tiger
- Inner Tiger
- Tan Tui
- Chang Ch'uan
- Bok Hok
- Leu Dong
- Fujien Gim/Sword
- Black Shantung Tiger Gim/Sword
- N. Saber/Yi Hae Mi Dao
- Double N. Saber
- Double S. Sabre

There are the forms of the Southern Crane Style our teacher learned, Wing Chun, multiple Crown Eagle Combat Forms, numerous rare internal sets (such as Taoist Golden Snake), and more. Low bows to my teacher—how did you achieve all this? To quote the Dao:

"The master does nothing, yet nothing is left undone."
Otherwise known as the Way of the Dragon.

Along with the forms are taught various traditional basics as required, such as traditional bows, specialized basics and fundamentals, applications, and the like in order to present all in a comprehensive and functional way.

Chin-na/Grappling Methods

5 Elements of Empty Handed Kung Fu

Despite their outer differences, Chinese Martial Arts are all made up of the same elements as diagramed above. Counters refers to the defenses / escapes one learns in the course of learning the other four major categories and the rest of the curriculum. Some styles may emphasize chin-na, such as Eagle Claw. Some kicking methods, such as Northern Shaolin. Others may emphasize grappling, such as Shuai Jiao. While other are famous for their hand techniques, such as Wing Chun. Regardless, to be effective and well-rounded each style and system must have some blend of these five.

Chin-na and grappling are a specialization in the Five Form Fist Shaolin system, with each of the main 5 sub-systems-Internal Arts, N.Shaolin, S.Shaolin, Ch'uan Fa, and Chinese

Weapons- having its own methods. In fact, Chin-na/Grappling is really like a sixth sub-system, as it is a study and curriculum unto itself.

My instructor, in addition to the Chinese styles and methods he learned, studied with renowned experts of diverse methods from other styles/cultures, such as Koichi Tohei, Wally Jay, Ken Ota, and Leo T. Gaje (who specialized in similar methods) This gives him a very deep and comprehensive knowledge and skill base. Of course his main teacher Dr. Daniel K. Pai, had tremendous knowledge of and skill with Chinese and Asian Chin-na/grappling methods.

At any rate in the "General Curriculum" chin-na/ grappling are taught in a very detailed and practical way. In the case of chin-na, the progression goes like this:

- Chin-na grips preformed on oneself (wrists)
- Applying these grips to a compliant partner
- Working these grips off of a punch, grab, or similar strike
- next the student learns several pre-set chin-na 2 person routines, which expand the skill-set and level of difficulty
- Chin-na is also incorporated into some of the pre-set self defense sets the student learns (wrist, elbow, shoulder, neck)
- The next level is Freestyle Chin-na utilizing 5-star Chin-na methods- working up to full speed and power.

Of course there is much more than this contained within the Five Form Fist System. My teacher is proficient in methods as diverse as Dragon, Tiger, Crown Eagle, and Taiji Na Fa. Crown Eagle is a chin-na system composed of 2 person chin-na sets which has been preserved by experts of the Koushu Federation, R.O.C. Taiji Na Fa refers to the specialized arts of gripping and holding/ controlling an opponent as employed in the internal art of Taiji Quan. Quite different than say, Shaolin Tiger Chin-na. As in most applications each art has its own unique flavor.

There are also other Chin-na methods besides those which control the joints. Including sealing the blood and breath, seizing the flesh/muscles/tendons and dim mak/tienhsueh. In the "General Curriculum" a bit of this is included, such as what we call the Japanese strangle hold (rear naked choke) and knowledge of vital points. A method of attacking vital points was shared with instructors which takes advantage of a system of lines on the body as well as time of day and angle/style of attack for the targets. That is the subject for another book, however.

As for the grappling arts, the Five Form Fist Shaolin System preserves very old and combat effective methods, which are distinct from modern Shuai Jiao. My teacher referred to his grappling arts as Gao Ti- literally, "horn butting" – which is a reference to an ancient brutal sport. Combatants would put on helmets and gore one another with the horns. The more common spelling for Gao Ti is Jiao Ti, which evolved into Jiao Li- ancient Chinese combat wrestling sans the horns and helmet. This is the art preserved here. The main difference with modern Shuai Jiao from what I can see is we never utilize high leg lifting sweeps and takedowns, nor do we bend over when we preform them , as done in Shuai Jiao. Maintaining balance on the field of combat is absolutely vital- the goal is no falls, ever!

The grappling methods in the "General Curriculum" are conveyed via various self-defense sets and methods, such as the Hidden Foot Maneuvers.

Key to both chin-na methods and grappling methods is enhanced knowledge and skill with all basics, especially footwork and hand skills; angle, range and zone (see chapter 2), anatomy, and principles of balance, leverage and energy transference. Internal arts such as Taiji and the Shaolin Butterfly style are naturals for these more advanced skills. In fact the symbol of the Shaolin Butterfly style and the one utilized in the great Prof. Wally Jays small circle jujitsuis one and the same- the Infinity Symbol. They share many of the same concepts and principles even though on the surface, they look so different.

Chinese Weapons

"The weapon hand trains the empty hand."- Ancient Kung Fu wisdom

Chinese weapons study is one of the five main sub-styles of Shaolin Five Form Fist, as the quote above implies, even though we may not rely on swords and spears very much nowadays for self-defense- much less national defense- they and the other weapons learned and studied still play a vital role in martial arts training.

Many empty hand techniques in fact owe their name to the type of energy and application they emulate from weapons training. Such as the "knife hand" "spear hand" "hammer fist" "spear kick" "sword hand" the "sword block" and the like. Thus training with these weapons and learning the weapon techniques they are named for is invaluable.

Additionally, training with weapons- solo and partner- requires greater levels of skill than empty hand martial arts requires and thus raises ones overall level of skill. When one can fight with weapons skillfully, fighting bare-handed is almost childs play (unless that child you are fighting with is Andre the Giant!). Training with weapons also can further develop key energies, principles, methods and techniques which are introduced in empty handed martial arts training. For instance, the first exercise taught in our 9 section steel whip training develops a very powerful central line (zhong ding) and the ability to transfer power from the central line to the hand and beyond, out through the tip of the weapon. This of course has numerous direct applications in empty hand martial arts.

Chinese weapons training, like Chinese culture and civilization, is ancient. Although there are literally thousands and thousands of Chinese weapons, some quite rare and exotic, there are four basic ones which are foundational to most Chinese martial systems and are also found commonly worldwide. Within these four there is quite a bit of variety, however, as there are numerous variations of these vital martial tools.

The four foundational weapons are the staff, spear, saber, and double-edged straight sword. Lets briefly examine these four weapons now. For a comprehensive and fascinating look at the history of ancient Chinese weapons, see <u>Ancient Chinese Weapons: A Martial Artists Guide, YMAA Publications, Jwing-Ming Yang.</u>

The Staff

The staff, or Gun in Chinese, Bo in Japanese (here in the United States "Bo Staff" is very commonly used, even by Chinese stylists) is often referred to as the grandfather of the weapons. Virtually all the martial styles have some version of it. In the Shaolin Five Form Fist system it is the first weapon taught. Training with the staff is a tremendous way to build whole body power, coordination of left and right side, upper and lower body, inner and outer, and breath and martial power. In our system we make use of both double end and single end staff methods- this is dictated by how one holds the staff- single end staff gives longer reach, double end more flexibility of the technique at medium and close range. The staff may also be tapered on one or both ends.

Staves may range from shoulder height to 9' long or longer. They are constructed of a variety of woods and materials, such as Chinese white waxwood, red oak, hickory, iron wood, rattan, bamboo, and other woods. The length of the staff and what it is made out of greatly determines how it is utilized. For instance a whip staff made of white waxwood and one made of iron (metal) will have quite different techniques.

Common staff techniques include:

- Striking Staff
- Thrusting Staff
- Blocking staff
- Deflecting staff
- Circling staff
- Shaking/Vibrating Staff

In the Shaolin Five Form Fist System "General Curriculum" students get a well-rounded introduction to this venerable weapon and its applications including:

- Break stance and ceremonial bow
- Double end/two handed blocks and single end deflections and drills
- Basic strikes and thrusts
- Solo and partner of above
- Simple self-defenses
- Monkey Stick Staff Form

Monkey stick is a fast moving and agile staff set with a plethora of excellent techniques which comes from a S.Crane style.

The staff is also an excellent weapon/tool for utilization as a training implement and yoga aid. In fact whole systems exist for these uses, such as Wizard Staff (Shamanic) and Dhanda Yoga, a staff based yoga system preserved and taught by Dr. Maung Gyi, Founder of the American Bando Association.

"Four Winds Staff Seminar," led by Dr. Maung Gyi, 2003

The monks of Shaolin were famed for their staff skills. Being Buddhists committed to non-violence originally it is taught that the staff—being a non-edged weapon—was the only one they would utilize. This of course was modified over time. Today Shaolin is famous for its numerous weapon styles.

The staff is also a symbol of spirituality, wisdom and power in both Eastern and Western cultures since ancient times.

The Saber/Broadsword

The Chinese saber has been the staple of the Chinese military and martial arts for centuries, utilized by the military right up until WWII and still today by Chinese stylists of virtually all Chinese styles. The saber or Dao (knife) is essentially a single-edged sword with a blade of varying thickness and curve. In Chinese culture a single-edge sword is referred to as a knife- some bigger, some smaller- a double-edged sword is what in their culture is recognized as a sword.

Sifu Dao Li Shen, don dau (saber)

There are numerous saber styles and designs: single hand and double hand; short, medium, and long handle style. It is a very powerful weapon which compared to some other weapons is easier to master- if you were to put in the work and maintain it. It is said that with 100, 8 hour training days one may master the basics of the saber. Of course due to the variety of styles one may train forever and still have more to learn.

Variations of the saber/broadsword include the Pu Dao or "horse chopper" which was widely utilized to attack the legs of the cavalry horses; the "butterfly swords"; the nine ring broadsword; and the famous Kwan Dao or "big knife"

Similar to the staff learning the saber in the "General Curriculum" of the Five Form Fist Shaolin system is a well-rounded affair, featuring the following:

- Break stance and ceremonial bow
- Basic saber strikes, blocks, deflections- in place and moving
- Simple partner drills
- Saber self-defense sets
- Forms: Fu Mei Don Dau S. Shaolin saber, then Yi Hae Mi Dao N. Shaolin saber; Southern and Northern double saber is also preserved.

The Spear

The Chinese spear or "Qiang" is known as the "king of the weapons," a devastating weapon on the battlefield and in personal combat. Spears were utilized by both infantry and by cavalry, the type/length of spear varying accordingly. Shorter spears were utilized by infantry and longer ones by cavalry. Spear length can vary from 7'-21'.

Shorter spears, 7'-9', were known also as "spiked staves." Medium spear would be in the 9'-13' foot range; long spear everything over 13'. Nowadays it is common to practice with a tapered white waxwood pole ending in a leaf shaped spearhead, and also sporting a red tassel. These are known as "flower spears" and are ideal for performance and also useful for light combat. The white waxwood staff is also known as a whip staff.

For the battlefield the "war spear" would feature a heavier type of wood, like an ironwood or heavy oak. The tassel is useful to attempt to distract an opponent, as well as to help stop blood from flowing down the shaft of the weapon so it does not become slippery to grip. Some styles/cultures also preserve something known as "hunting spear", which as the name suggests is for obtaining sustenance not for self-defense so much (against humans anyway). In Filipino "hunting spear" all of the techniques are done either vertically or thrusting- in the native jungle environment there is no room for lateral/circling motions or techniques.

The main techniques are thrusting/stabbing, slashing, sweeping and blocking/deflecting. Notable methods include holding the staff with one hand for full extension and reach, and large circling/sweeping motions to keep attackers at distance. There are numerous variations of the basic techniques with footwork and attacks/deflections for all angles. In the Chinese style and traditions the spear is rarely thrown.

It is said that it takes 1,000 days (8 hours per day) to master the uses of the Chinese spear.

The staff is a foundational weapon for the spear. A variation is the halberd (ji) which is like a spear with the addition of either one or two crescent shaped blades at the end of the weapon, utilized to slash as well as to entrap opponents lighter weapons.

The Sword

The Chinese double-edged straight sword or "Jian/Ch'ien" in Mandarin and "Gim" as she is known in Cantonese, is known as the "Queen of the Weapons." Here again there are quite a few variations, the main ones being known as the "scholar sword" and the "warrior sword." Outwardly they are similar, featuring a handle, guard and a double edged blade. The 'Scholar Sword" however would have a semi-flexible blade or one with gradations of flexibility- the third near the handle being rigid and unsharpened, the middle third being semi-flexible and sharpened; the last third very thin and flexible, almost like a razor blade. Each third of the blade was utilized for different types of technique- blocking/deflecting; hacking or razor-like, pinpoint thrusts, cuts, and slashes (from 1st to last third of the blade).

The "Scholar Sword" was also known as the "Female Sword" or "Yin Sword", and was often associated with nobility or high social status. It was not the weapon of the common soldier. Nowadays it is often associated with Chinese Internal Styles, such as Taiji; and is an elegant yet deadly weapon (in the right hands).

The "Warrior Sword" featured a rigid and heavier blade, useful on the battlefield and even able to pierce armor, but perhaps a bit less sophisticated. It is also known as the "Male Sword" or the "Yang Sword" due to its properties and techniques and tactics. "Warrior Swords" featured a "blood groove" down the center of the blade which allowed it to be withdrawn if thrust into the body of an opponent (the wound seals around the blade, the blood groove breaks the seal somewhat).

The "Scholar Sword" would often also feature a tassle attached to the handle, useful as a training tool to develop balance and skill in utilizing the weapon; as well as to distract an opponent. Combat versions of the tassel might be made of metal/steel filaments which contained hooks.

The guard of older versions of these swords generally was shaped like an upside down half-circle. This protected the hand from the opponent's blade. More modern styles of the handle feature an upturned handle U, which also protects the grip hand but has the added feature of being able to hook the opponent's blade.

Blade lengths can vary from 18" to 32" or more. Longer, heavier jian would feature two-handed technique (2 hands on the handle). The jian also features single grips and various specialized reinforced grips and finger grips. The empty-hand/

off-hand often employs a hand posture known as the "secret sword hand". It is like the famous "peace sign" except with the index and middle fingers joined. "The Occult" or "Secret Sword Hand" balances the flow of energy through the arms and sword, and is also trained to deliver deadly close range "dim mak" type attacks. This is somewhat similar to a "sword and knife" style sans the knife.

Like the saber/ broadsword there is also double-sword, though this is less common. Due to the double edge nature of the weapon wielding two at once is challenging, only those very skilled should attempt this (with sharpened swords anyway).

Due to the sophistication of the weapon and the difficulty in mastering all of its nuances it is said that it takes 10,000 days to master its uses- 30 years! Needless to say there are very few true sword experts left, in the true sense of the meaning of mastery as dictated by traditional standards.

The following is a comparison of some of the characteristics of the Jian (sword) and Dao (saber):

Properties	Sword	Saber
Time	10,000 days to master	100 days to master
Animal	Phoenix/Dragon	Tiger
Color	Blue	Black/Red
Rank	Nobility/Scholar	Combat/Soldier
Element	Spiritual/Heaven	Earth
Use	Scalpel	Cleaver

The double-edged straight sword is also traditionally a symbol for the arts in general, and our use of them. It is said the art (like a sword) can cut for us, cutting us free from attachments and difficulties; or it can cut against us, hurting ourselves by misuse.

Together the sword and the saber symbolize Heaven and Earth, Yin and Yang, Tiger and Dragon, and are featured in many schools, temples and homes where Chinese martial arts are practiced (often in a crossed swords/sabers and shield motif).

In the Five Formed Fist "General Curriculum" students are first exposed to the sword bow and salutation, basics and drills-solo and partner. Later form and self-defense is added. The first forms taught are Fujian Jian/Sword and black Shantung Tiger Jian/Sword.

As mentioned there are literally thousands of weapons which have been developed and utilized throughout Chinese martial and military history. Some of the more common ones include:

- Nine section steel whip
- Monk's spade
- Hook swords
- Emei piercers
- Bow and arrow/Crossbow
- Spikes/stars
- Blowgun
- Meteor Hammer/Rope Dart
- Tiger fork
- Trident
- Daggers
- Hammers/bludgeons
- Wind/fire wheels
- Many others

Sparring/free-fighting Training

Sparring practice and training is an essential part of a student's development in the art of Shaolin Five Form Fist. The "General Curriculum" contains a variety of sparring methods and "Graduated Sparring Drills" so that students of all ages, fitness levels, and eagerness for (or not for) contact sparring can safely participate.

There is nothing random about the training, not initially anyway. First off, beginning level students are not allowed to spar. The idea here being that one must first gain familiarity and basic skills with the art and its methods before one can attempt to spar. This process is very similar to learning to drive a car. One starts out with very simple lessons, in the driveway and classroom, before driving in the street. And even then one begins driving slow, low traffic backstreets- not rush hour traffic in Los Angeles!

Similarly, a student begins with simple- but essential- drills like punching/blocking and kicking/blocking with a partner. There are specialized drills for each of the methods taught, many of them- stationary and moving. From here the student progresses to various methods of "step sparring". "Step Sparring" is a method of practice which is very wide- spread amongst Asian martial arts in various forms and known by a variety of names depending on culture, language, and martial art style.

They are essentially drills which allow students to practice a form of "pre-arranged" or "pre-set" sparring, making use of the basic techniques they are learning. As the student progresses the "step sparring" can also progress, becoming more challenging, and may encompass grappling and takedowns as well as striking/blocking.

An example of a simple "step-sparring" drill would be to have 2 students face each other in ready stance. Student A steps forward and delivers a Ram's Head (reverse) punch. Student B steps back and deflects it with a palm block, then counter- punches to students A's sternum with his own Ram's Head punch and releases a Tiger Shout/Kiai simultaneous with the timed landing of the punch. Similar methods are practiced for 2 step sparring, 3 steps and more.

These drills begin slowly in order to develop coordination and confidence, then progress to full speed and power. Advanced students are encouraged to utilize "fighting energy", to perform them as if their hair was on fire and their life depended on it. Each drill is taught in a formal way, with the Sifu issuing verbal commands, beating the drum, and the students responding with the Spirit Shout, Tiger Shout or Snake Breath as needed.

So "Step-Sparring" performs many vital functions, and can be quite enjoyable. Skills developed include:

- Stance and footwork
- Timing
- Distance and Spacing
- Rhythm
- Speed
- Flow
- Focus
- Delivery of power
- Coordination- all techniques, as well as mind, breath/ chi, and the technique

Similar drills exist for weapons training later in the students training. There are also "flow drills" and "chaining drills."

Now, drills are important but it is vital that the student progresses to free-style sparring as soon as possible. Step-sparring and other simple drills can build a false sense of skill and accomplishment. Even drills with randomness and a more free-style aspect built into them are still drills. Both street combat/self-defense, and warfare- the battlefield- are anything but "pre-set". In fact, they can be downright chaotic and mercilessly unpredictable. F.U.B.A.R, for real.

Of course, much of the same can be said for even the heaviest full-contact sparring/fighting- even this isn't the same as the street or the jungle or the battlefield. However, even light free-style sparring is a better test and approximation than simple pre-set step drills are. Thus, sparring is an invaluable tool for developing "for real" self-defense skills.

Students are trained in 3 main modes of sparring:

1.Slow Speed- Sometimes called "taiji speed" sparring, which allows students the time to defend and attack safely and with fore thought—without fear of being hit very hard, or at all.

2. Medium speed – Like the name suggests, both the tempo and power are upped till the students are sparring at about half speed/power.

3. Full Speed/power- This level is reserved for students that are ready for it, no pulling of the punches or kicks, all techniques may be utilized.

Other sparring methods include:

Restricted techniques: One student may be restricted to a small set of techniques, say front punch, front kick, circle block; and the other student to a similar set of restricted techniques- say, backfist, sidekick, forearm block

Offense/defense: Here the students take turns- one offense only, one defense only. This may be mixed with the restricted techniques method as well.

Sparring Circle: Here the students form a circle with one student in the center. The student in the center spars with students chosen at random by the Sifu. After a time, a new student takes the center position and spars with multiple partners chosen by the Sifu. The longest I saw a student last was one hour straight non-stop in the center fighting full-contact with one fresh partner after another. By the end he was essentially a human punching bag, but he hung in there and proved himself to be a true and worthy student.

Living the Art

"The art which you can see- the strikes, forms, fighting and the like- is only the tip of the tip of the iceberg in relation to the true and total art." – Guro Dan Inosanto

Shaolin Five Form Fist and the Butterfly style were taught to us as total life arts. Traditional martial arts offer so much more than the common, public understanding and are so misunderstood. The symbol of my teacher's school and art is the White Lotus. The White Lotus is a sacred spiritual symbol known all over Asia, and symbolizes the flowering of the individual on the Path. No matter who we are, no matter where we come from- even from the lowest, dirtiest muck and filth- with discipline and guidance from within and without we can transform ourselves and achieve the pinnacle of self-realization, enlightenment, or union with God. Or whatever similar words you have for the highest human achievement.

The principles, concepts, and methods which we learn about in training, things such as: respect, wisdom, power, control, self-awareness, compassion, teamwork, family, timing, focus, discipline, and so much more- apply not only in the microcosmic world of the kwoon, dojo, or training hall; but in the macrocosm of our lives. My teacher would always encourage us to "never put the art down for long" and to use it to "fight and win all of the battles in our lives." He emphasized that the most important time to practice the art, in fact, was in the "kwoon of daily life." Interestingly, my Buddhist teacher taught us the same thing, saying the most important time to practice the art was to live it during what he called "the meditation break," meaning the time in between our sessions with him.

Having had a very challenging life since birth, these teachings and others like it I encountered along the way were literally life-saving and transforming. The only way to properly thank my teacher is to attempt to live as he taught us and pass it on to others.

Of course, all of the true, traditional teachers teach in much the same way, regardless of the culture. In the Chinese tradition this is called "Wu De" or "Martial Morality." It is Wu De which makes the martial arts, arts of living- not merely pugilism.

So, Wu De is like a code of ethics and virtues, and includes both guidelines for the mind/thoughts, and words/deeds. Again, this mirrors exactly how I was taught. I asked my teacher once what the purpose of Taiji Quan was. He answered, "to redirect, neutralize, and/or transform negativity of word, thought and deed." Perfect.

Classically, Wu De as taught in the Chinese traditions includes the following:

<u>Morality of Deed</u>
- Humility
- Respect
- Righteousness
- Trust
- Loyalty

These are sometimes given as:
- Respect
- Humility
- Trust
- Virtue
- Honor

<u>Morality of Mind</u>-
- Will
- Endurance
- Perseverance
- Patience
- Courage

The Chinese speak of bringing the "emotional mind" or Xin into harmony with the "wisdom mind" or Hui. This emphasizes a maturation of the individual, guided by classical virtues such as:

- Temperance
- Prudence
- Courage
- Justice

Again, these teachings are traditionally universal. I remember at a Chinese New Years celebration at a wonderful local Chinese restaurant some years ago, which included lion dancing and kung Fu performances. I was having a conversation with 2 of the owner's most lovely and beautiful daughters (he and his wife had 4 daughters which each was like a Chinese Playboy centerfold, and their son was like a Chinese Arnold Schwarzenegger!). So I am speaking to these 2 beautiful girls, but being very respectful given the setting and they were the owners daughters- and they looked at each other and burst out laughing saying, "all of the kung fu guys are the same!" Ahh, good old Wu De, you have it, or you don't. It's unmistakable.

At any rate, the arts and Wu De having been practiced and refined for so long now are completely intertwined. Witness the "Kung Fu Salute," which along with the "Break Stance" my teacher taught contained the entire art in a seed form. One of the basic meanings of the Kung Fu salute is "control over power." So while it is indeed martial technique, simultaneously it is Wu De. Genius!

Along with these traditional teachings on Wu De, my teacher shared some which are unique to our lineage. Such as the teachings of <u>The Dragon</u>:

- Wisdom
- Courage
- Honor
- Strength
- Purity
- All Knowledge

The Dragon being a symbol of the practitioner in our system, as is the Butterfly.

Living the art manifests in countless ways. We were taught to be spiritual warriors, thus to view each step, each breath, every moment of every day as both a test and a lesson. Being respectful and kind, wise and honorable, courageous and strong is needed not only in life's big, dramatic episodes- but all the time, everywhere, Such as the line in the grocery store. Washing the dishes. Family gatherings. At work. Dealing with strangers. For challenging people and those whom are a delight to be around. As the old wisdom says,

"As iron sharpens iron, so one man sharpens another."

I'd like to end this section with a beautiful and inspiring poem by Prof. Li Shixin of Beijing University. Prof. Li is a noted author on the Chinese martial arts and acknowledged expert. This was shared with me by one of his students (Mr. David Schneider):

Tai Chi is eternal.
No boundary, no frontier.
As tall as the sky.
As deep as the earth.
It may not be seen.
It may not be touched.
To seek the Tai Chi path
Is to seek purity itself.
May the path be the guide,
To the unfathomable depths.

-Prof. Li Shixin

Chapter Five: Shaolin Butterfly Curriculum

General Description

So far we have been exploring the Shaolin Butterfly Style from a number of angles. To sum up:

- It has its own unique history and lineage which is born from the history and lineage of Chinese Martial Arts in general and Shaolin in particular
- It is a "High/Internal Style" of Chinese Shaolin Kung Fu
- It has its own unique concepts, principles, and philosophies and also shares many utilized by all martial arts
- As we have detailed, The Shaolin Butterfly Style exists as a sub-style within a much larger martial system, the White Lotus Shaolin Five Form Fist
- In fact, it occupies an important and key place in the system as the "Inner Connector Style"
- Additionally, traditionally the Shaolin Five Form Fist "General Curriculum" has served as the foundation curriculum for the Shaolin Butterfly Style, which was reserved for Sifu-level disciples and not taught publicly

Now we will detail out in text and photo the specific material and curriculum which make up the Shaolin Butterfly Style, as it was taught and described to me. Briefly, as in any specific style, it has its own unique basic methods, concepts and principles, forms and applications. There are 3 open-hand forms: 2 open hand, solo forms and one 2 person combat form.

Although it has no weapons forms, the larger system it is a part of has many weapons forms and applications. In 2013 I created a saber form based upon concepts of the Butterfly and Dragon and internal arts as I understood them, the "Butterfly Bagua/Taiji Dao" Set—utilizing a long ring-handle Taiji Dao (saber). I performed this set at the New England World Martial Arts Championship and was cheered on completion, finishing second in musical forms, men's 30 and over (I was 49). The form was executed virtually flawlessly but I didn't have the music right. At any rate, this set is of my own creation and not a traditional part of the style as described and passed on to me.

Progression of learning

We were taught, as previously described, in a very traditional way. We began with the key, foundation "seed techniques" and drilled them very slowly for quite some time. Being an Internal Style this was slow, meditative work focused on breathing and linking mind/chi/body/technique together. This happens via the linkages between the Dan Tien and Consciousness which the breath facilitates.

A "seed technique" is just like it sounds—a technique which holds in a latent, dormant form an entire class of techniques, or even an entire style or system.

Once our teacher was satisfied with our progress with these 3 simple methods, we then moved on to performing them while slowly stepping forward, then backwards. We did this stepping utilizing the well known "dan-tien ma" or "dan-tien stance," known by many as the hour-glass stance or san chin stance. "San chin" is known in Cantonese as "Saam Jin" or "Saam Chin," in Mandarin as "San Chan," and in the Fujian dialect as, "San Chien." San chin is the name utilized for both the stance and numerous versions of the seminal kata/kuen in Okinawan and Japanese styles.

This leads me to believe that perhaps this Shaolin Butterfly Style was developed from Southern Shaolin teachings and techniques, as does the lack of acrobatics. But this is mere speculation, as Northern styles also make use of the "dantien ma/san chin" stance, and after all, Taiji is a Northern style originally. In fact, the "San Chan" is as old as Shaolin herself, as Bodhidharma (Damo) created various meditative/exercise/Qi Gong sets which make use of the stance. In our system there is a set preserved which is called "Damo's Muscle Change Classic" which makes good use of the "San Chan" or san chin.

Once the stepping forward and backward is learned well and coordinated smoothly and naturally with the 3 seed hand techniques then additional Butterfly hand techniques and drills are learned. From here the progression moves to partner drills and applications; then utilizing the techniques in sparring. We also worked on bound-wrist Butterfly technique and drills (binding our wrists with flexible, strong rope).

This material was originally taught to us in closed-door Sifu level Instructor classes over a period of about a year. Notice not only did we not start with forms, we didn't even learn one! We all already knew many forms so we were taught what was most important—the foundation from the "seeds" on up to the roots and trunk. That being strong and healthy serves as the foundation for the rest.

Some years later my teacher opened up and taught some public workshops on this rare and superb style. It was here that he introduced a short-form version of the first form in the curriculum "The Butterfly Energy Form."

Let's look at these "seed techniques" now.

The "seed techniques" are very versatile. They can be held as standing Nei Gong postures; practiced slowly with breathing and internal focus and awareness as Qi Gong; and practiced solo or with a partner as martial arts.

The 3 Seed Techniques and Drills

Being an Internal Style, the training in Shaolin Butterfly Style begins very much like beginning learning in a traditional Taiji style: simple, slow meditative movements. This performs many, many important functions, such as:

- Release of extraneous tensions of mind and body—there are many, many levels of this, all the way to the core of our being, known classically as "fang song gong"
- Uniting mind, technique, energy, dan-tien, and root—this happens via utilizing breathing methods and internal focus/external focus in a certain way which allows this to happen—known classically as "Yi-Qi-Li"
- Refinement of the "central line" of energy in the body, a key practice which is said to be so important it is "the first thing, and the last thing" one keeps refining. A beginner generally has very little connection to and awareness of this "central line," while a true expert will have one that is as refined, vibrant and powerful as a laser beam. This is one of the ways true martial art masters and spiritual masters can recognize each other—mastery of the "central line," which has many names. In the practice of Chinese internal martial arts the practice of refining and perfecting the "central line" is part of what is known as "zhong ding" or "central equilibrium."

Various names for the "central line":
- The Central Channel
- Zhong Mai
- Sushumna
- Core Channel
- Avadhuti
- RtsaDbu Ma

- The inner, metaphysical aspect of the Central Channel is known as the "silver cord" or "sutratma" (the life thread of the antahkarana)
- Inner and Outer Balance and Harmony
- Refining various principles, such as Yang Cheng Fu's "10 Important Points," my teacher emphasized <u>3 Essential Principles</u> which when one gained skill with activated other principles 1) Suspend the Headtop 2) Center in the Dan Tien 3) Root in the Feet

So one begins practicing these 3 Seed Techniques in place, slowly, with a particular method of breathing and meditative focus. This must be learned in person. Formally one stands upright and performs the Break Stance/Kung Fu Salute:

From here there are a number of ways to step into the dan-tien ma or san chin stance and raise the hands to Seed Technique #1:

Next on exhalation one lowers the hands to position #2 and forms Seed Technique #2:

Note there is a particular breathing method and focus which is combined with the exercise, which is a variation of something known as the "Mind Triangle."

So we started with this simple exercise for hours and weeks on end, stepping into position #1 and breathing in, exhaling and moving to position #2, then inhaling and moving to position #1 again. First with the right hand/wrist over the left, then switching to the left over the right. Very slow, focused, meditative work.

After a time Seed Technique #3 was added, what I call the "Butterfly Palm Change." The Butterfly Palm Change (B.P.C.) is the key to the entire art, the physical embodiment of the Infinity Symbol, the Symbol of the Butterfly Style ∞.

To perform the B.P.C., after performing Seed Technique #2, as one inhales to raise the hands one turns the palms inwards (rotating the wrists without disengaging them) pointing the fingers towards the face at about mouth/nose level. One then rotates the arms/wrists back to position/Seed Technique #1— but now the other wrist is on top!

This becomes the key, foundational Butterfly Drill:

- Step to Position/Seed Technique #1
- Exhale move to Position/Seed Technique #2
- Inhale, perform the Butterfly Palm Change, Seed Technique #3
- Now the other wrist is on top in Position/Seed Technique #1
- Repeat—over and over
- One may also just practice Seed Techniques #1 and #2 without the Butterfly Palm Change for a serious of 3, 5, 10, 20 repetitions—then perform the Butterfly Palm Change for another 3, 5, 10, 20 repetitions (or what have you) with the other wrist on top.

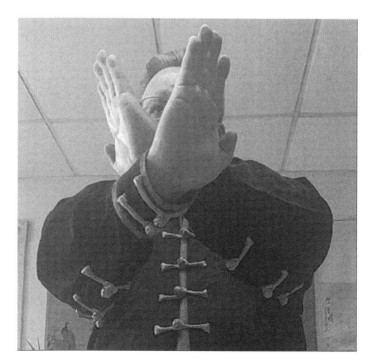

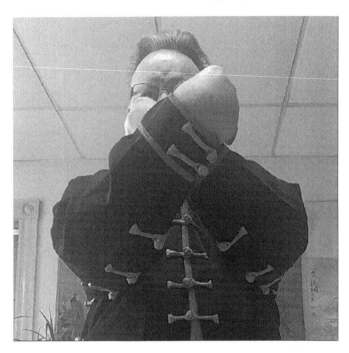

After a period of time, step back to the beginning Break Stance/Kung Fu Salute Position and take a break. There are a number of ways of doing this formally.

Once these methods have been learned well one progresses to stepping forward and backwards in the san chin/san chan/ saam chien stance—one foot slightly ahead of the other, toes pointed inward, knees about one fist width apart and the tailbone tucked under (take the curve out of the lower spine).

As you step forward or backwards utilizing the small, circular stepping method particular to the san chin step one performs the Butterfly Palm Change, inhaling and raising the hands from Position/Seed Technique #2. As one settles into the new stance (one step forward or backward) the hands are lowered down to Position/Seed Technique #2 again. Repeat. Think of it as an Inward Deflection as you step forward or backward (this, in fact, is one of the applications).

We again focused on just this stepping pattern for quite some time as it is an essential, foundation method. Many other stepping methods combined with Butterfly Techniques are possible, such as the Lotus Steps, circle walking Butterfly Style, and the various foundational methods of our system.

Foundational Butterfly Methods
-The Butterfly Ready Stance

So these methods are the key, essential and foundational "Seed Techniques." Let's explore some of the other unique and interesting Butterfly Techniques and Methods now.

We could also call this the Butterfly Guard Position. It is a posture one may begin various drills and exercises from, pause in, or utilize to perform self-defense maneuvers with a partner with. A left or right lead stance may also be utilized and either hand may be on top. As the fingers are pointed upwards towards the sky this is a "Yang" Butterfly Palm Formation. Seed Technique #1, fingers pointing downward towards the earth, is a "Yin" Butterfly Palm Formation. This formation is very useful as a deflection versus strikes or grabs, and for various chin-na maneuvers and escapes.

Now, many of the Butterfly techniques are practiced fitting into the basic seed techniques Butterfly Palm Change Drill. So as one practices the seed techniques #1, #2, and the B.P.C. #3—after the B.P.C. one performs another technique—such as the reinforced Butterfly Punch—then goes back to the seed techniques Butterfly Palm Change Drill. While many of the Butterfly Techniques have the hands/wrists/palms/fists united in various unique ways, they aren't always—the hands do indeed separate, only to unite again.

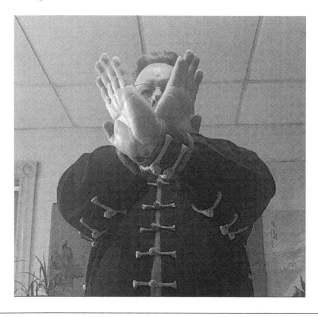

Obviously in combat one's hands must be free to react as needed. The Butterfly practice of performing the seed techniques drill and inserting other techniques into it—with the joined hands separating then uniting again—is what begins to form the Infinity Symbol internally and energetically, in mind and body (along with various other specialized drills, which we shall describe).

After some time with good discipline and effort, contemplation and application, one no longer has a left side and a right side. They transcend this duality and become fully integrated, forming something new. Just as the wings of a hawk must be fully integrated for it to fly so beautifully and powerfully, just so the left and right sides of the Butterfly Stylist become integrated. We become a graceful, powerful, and deadly human Butterfly!w

Each of the following techniques may be inserted into the basic seed techniques Butterfly Palm Change Drill:

-Reinforced Butterfly Punch

This is a close to mid-range technique which can be drilled within the format of the basic seed techniques Butterfly Palm Change drill. After performing seed technique #2 as one raises the palms and performs the B.P.C., rather than forming seed technique #1, one forms the reinforced Butterfly Punch. To get back to the drill, one performs another B.P.C. and continues on. Of course, one can also practice this technique in a variety of other drills, including with a partner in graduated self-defense applications and sparring drills.

This technique is very versatile and may be part of an escape from a grip, converted into an actual chin-na technique in its own right, and utilized in a close range pushing/striking fashion. These are in addition to its obvious striking applications.

-Reinforced Butterfly Double Palm

Just as above, this technique can fit into the basic seed techniques B.P.C. drill. Here, as one performs the B.P.C. instead of forming seed technique #1, one performs the reinforced double palm. Then to get back to the drill one performs the B.P.C. and returns to seed techniques #1 and #2 as the hands rise and fall. All the time the breath is coordinated with the movements.

-Butterfly Double Reinforced Spear Hands

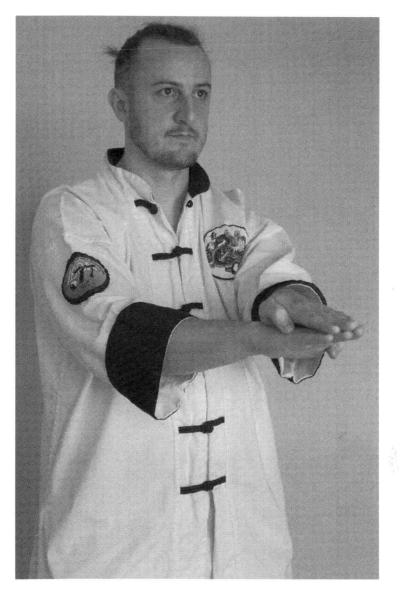

This technique is practiced the same as the previous ones in the context of the B.P.C. drill with the seed techniques.

<u>-Reinforced Middle-Gate Butterfly Palm Blocks</u>

This technique is practiced the same as the previous ones in the context of the B.P.C. drill with the seed techniques. When the right wrist is over the left, after performing the B.P.C. the left hand will reinforce the right at the right side middle-gate. Reverse it when the left is on top to begin.

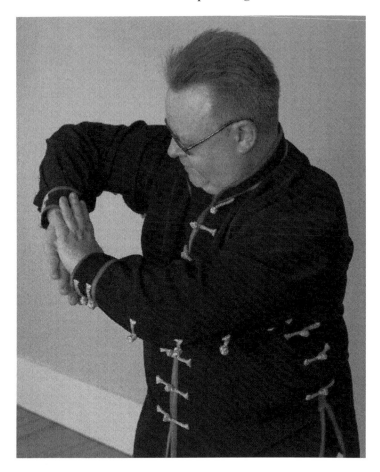

-Butterfly Crossed Forearm Blocks

This technique is practiced the same as the previous ones in the context of the B.P.C. drill with the seed techniques. When the right hand is on top the left forearm will reinforce the right as shown; switch it if the left is on top as you begin the B.P.C. This technique in application can be executed to the right or left middle and lower gates, and the front lower or upper gate and is very useful versus powerful leg attacks.

-B.P.C. Inside Deflection

This technique is hidden within the B.P.C. itself, in the form of the fingers pointing towards the face position.

In addition to being useful as an inside deflection it has applications for chin-na and escapes.

-Double Butterfly Circle Palms

This technique is drilled the same as many of the others in the context of the basic B.P.C. drill with the seed techniques. When the right hand is on top perform the B.P.C., the hands separate, with the left circling high to low outside to the left, and the right circling low to high outside to the right. They rejoin in the front center (right still on top) and you begin the B.P.C. drill with the seed techniques again. Switch all of this if you begin the B.P.C. drill with the left hand on top.

Other Butterfly Techniques include:

-Butterfly Wings

These are similar to Crane's Wings Techniques except that in practice the fingers are bit softer and formed a bit differently. In application one uses the amount of hardness/softness needed to get the job done.

There are three basic Butterfly Wing Formations:

-To the sides:

-<u>Front to back:</u>

-And double to the front:

These can also be performed in the context of the basic Butterfly Palm Change Drill with seed techniques #1, #2, and

#3 (the B.P.C.). Like all of these techniques they can also be practiced with a partner in various ways, including attack/defense applications and sparring.

-Butterfly Joined Palm Techniques

These methods are somewhat similar to the well-known "Buddhist Palm" techniques, though performed with the Butterfly flavor, style, and energy. Bringing the palms together as in "prayer position" is another unique way of joining left and right for a variety of techniques and training methods. The joined palms may be pointing fingers up vertically; or pointing forward with the joined palms horizontal, and even downwards or to either side. They may move in all directions, including circles, and are useful for a variety of strikes and deflections. Like the joined wrist methods, the joined palms can separate and join at will anytime as needed.

A variation is for the palm heels to join with the fingertips of one hand pointing up and those of the other down, in a yin-yang joined Butterfly Palm formation (this technique is famously made use of in Hung Gar Form, "Taming the Tiger").

Other basic techniques are single and double Butterfly Ridge Hand Strikes. We initially learned these as part of a "Butterfly Throw Hands" drill, but of course they can be practiced in other ways as well (such as in the B.P.C. drill).

There are a number of other basic Butterfly Techniques but they are best left for video. The above described methods give you a good view into the Butterfly Style. As for drills, there are a variety of solo and partner drills beyond the ones described above, which again due to intricacy are best left for video. The most important of these is repetition of the Butterfly Palm Change all by itself, over and over, sans the seed techniques #1 and #2. As with all techniques, but especially this one, it needs to be practiced many thousands of times just to become natural—hundreds of thousands of times to master. This drill is also practiced with a partner versus grabs and punches.

Another key drill begins in the Butterfly Ready Stance, the Butterfly Palm Horizontal Circle Drill:

One shifts the weight left and right slowly while the Yang Butterfly Palms make a horizontal circle. As you shift left the Butterfly Palms circle outward to the left, then inward to the body. As you shift to the right they move to the right close to the body, then outward and to the left again as you shift left.

Dr. Maung Gyi told me how my teacher many years ago as the live-in disciple and Chief Instructor of Dr. Daniel K. Pai would practice the Butterfly Palm Change Drill incessantly. In fact, when I first mentioned this rare Shaolin Style to great-grandmaster Dr. Maung Gyi he stopped dead in his tracks and asked me to show him, then shared this story with me. We were in the parking lot of an American Kenpo School that he was going to teach at (I drove him). Later on a break he had me demonstrate the Butterfly Energy Short Form for the students assembled, and directed them all to learn from me. Needless to say the school owner didn't like that part.

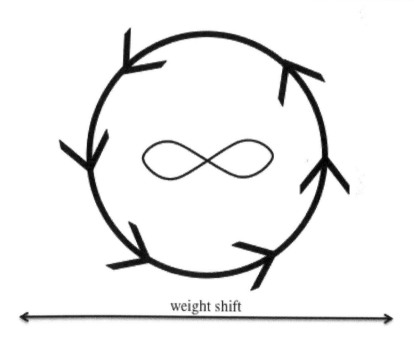

weight shift

Circle Drill Beginning to Left
You just reverse this for the clockwise circle by beginning shifting to the right:

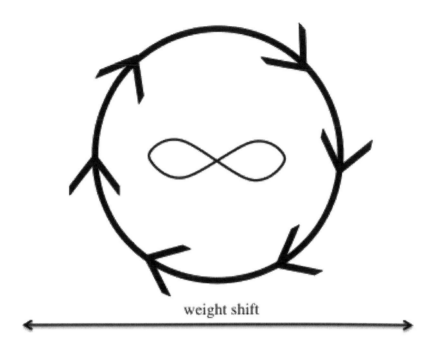

weight shift

Circle Drill Beginning to Right

Butterfly Applications

Let's look at some simple 2 person applications of these Butterfly Techniques now:

Here is a sample application of the opening posture of the first form in the curriculum, the Butterfly Energy Form (more on that in a bit):

While this posture is also useful as an introspective and nurturing standing nei gung/meditation posture, it also has applications, here as the foundation of an Interlocking Arm-Lock, as the following series of photographs shows:

Here is a sample application utilizing the crossed wrist Yang Butterfly Palm position to deflect a punch and perform another arm-lock/chin-na maneuver:

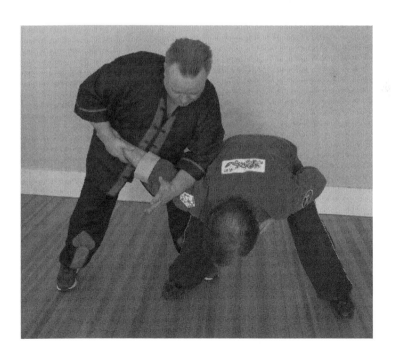

This is a sample application showing how the Butterfly Palms can be utilized to escape from a grab, then for a counter I utilized the reinforced Butterfly Punch to the bottom of the sternum.

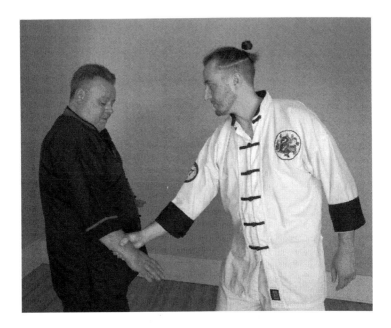

Here is an application making use of the Butterfly Inside Deflection, followed up with a double reinforced palm strike:

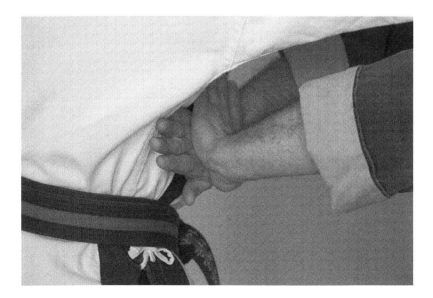

This is a similar application making use of the Butterfly Inside Deflection off of a punch, this time followed up with a double reinforced spear hand strike to the bottom of the throat:

Here is a Butterfly Wing application versus a front thrust kick. The right Butterfly Wing has deflected and trapped the kick as the left one strikes/wards the opponent off; the left then traps the back of the neck as the right circles up and down to counter. This application is taken directly from the first set, the Butterfly Energy Form:

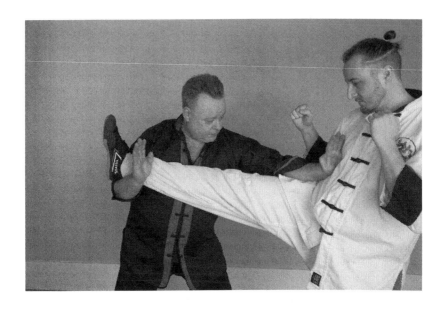

Here is another Butterfly Wing application, this time versus a front punch, showing how the wings can open from the crossed position then together again utilizing the principle of the Infinity Symbol ∞:

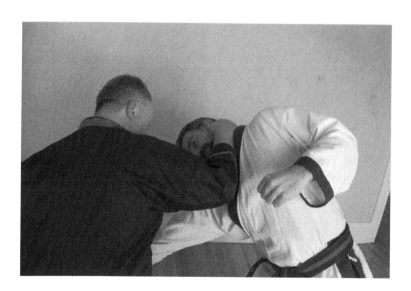

This application demonstrates how the double Butterfly Palms may be utilized, coming together, separating, and countering:

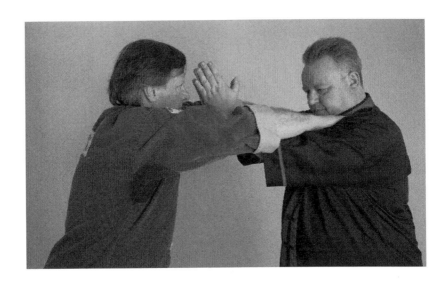

This is another application utilizing the Butterfly Palms to escape from a grab, then stepping in and countering with an elbow to the ribs:

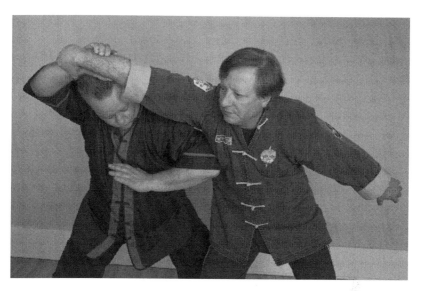

This is a simple application versus a double grab and attempted knee strike, utilizing the Butterfly Palms—from here one may follow-up in any number of ways:

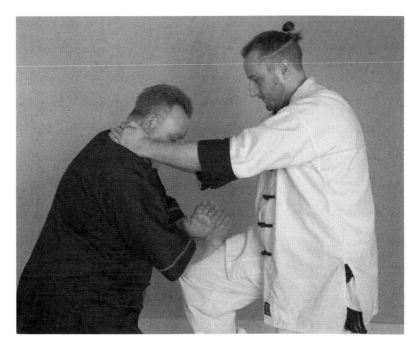

This application utilizes the Butterfly Inside Deflection off of a punch, then the hands separate to simultaneously counter-strike and deflect a second hand attack:

This application demonstrates the use of the crossed-Butterfly Forearm Block versus a roundhouse kick attack, stopping the kicking leg and then trapping it—from there any number of more counters may happen, including various takedowns:

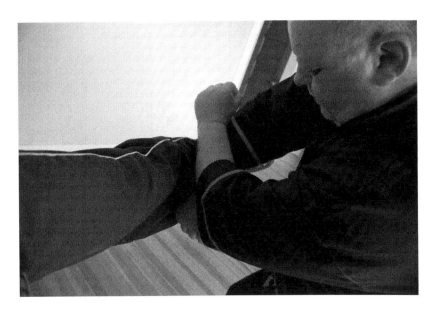

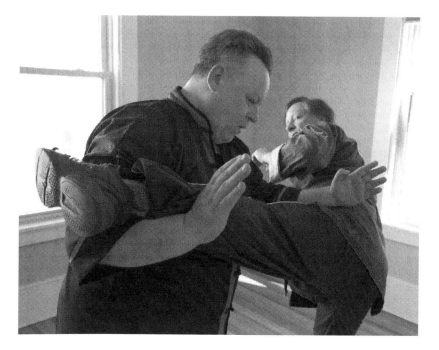

So these simple Butterfly applications should give you an idea of how the techniques can work in a basic fashion. I hope to produce a video to act as a companion to this book, in which case we would be able to show more clearly how this style looks and applies itself.

Shaolin Butterfly Forms

As mentioned, there are 3 forms which are included in this style. Let's briefly examine them now:

Form #1: The Butterfly Energy Form

As the Shaolin Butterfly Style is what is known as an "Internal" style of Chinese martial arts, the training begins slowly, softly, meditatively, and meticulously. The same is true for the forms training. In fact this first set I often refer to as "Butterfly Taiji,"

as it is virtually indistinguishable from that art, albeit a somewhat exotic version of it.

I was taught a short-form version of the long form. It contains all manner of solo and joined hand Butterfly techniques, leg maneuvers and kicks, single and double-weighted stances.

Here are a few sample photographs of postures from the Butterfly Energy Form:

crossed arms

butterfly palms look right

stop hit and chamber punch

Butterfly Crane

Circling Butterfly Palms

Form #2: Butterfly Bound Wrist Set Solo Form

So this set is performed with the wrists bound. It is practiced at a faster speed than the Butterfly Energy Form, with speed and power. This is a direct carry-over from the origin of the style, a Shaolin expert jailed with wrists tied behind his back.

In fact, the form begins this way. The first movement is to squat and hop, bringing the bound wrists/hands under the feet and in front of the body. From here it proceeds to all manner of bound wrist/hand techniques.

Form #3: Butterfly Combat (2 Person) Form

So this set is Set #2, the bound-wrist solo set, performed with a partner whose hands are not bound. This further perfects the skill of defending oneself with bound/joined wrists.

Obviously this is not a position we would want to find ourselves in. As a training method, however, it is superb. When combined with the non-bound Butterfly training it makes a great contribution towards perfecting the Butterfly technique and skill. And, of course, should you ever find yourself in a situation where your wrists are tied together and you have to fight, you will be ready!!

Butterfly Techniques in Other Styles

As we mentioned earlier in the book, while Butterfly Styles are extremely rare, many styles contain Butterfly techniques and/or concepts. Sometimes they are explicitly referred to as Butterfly techniques—like the Butterfly Palms of the Hung Gar and the Butterfly Kicks (standing and ground Butterfly Kicks). Sometimes they are not, but none-the-less fit the Butterfly Concept—such as the X-Blocks of various karate styles (and Shaolin styles).

Essentially, in a basic form, the Butterfly Concept is the use of the joined wrists/palms/hands. Virtually all styles have techniques like this, from Ji/Press in Taiji to the reinforced grips in Kali.

Here are some pictures from other styles of techniques/posture, which fit into the Butterfly Concept:

The Butterfly Style and technique also very easily combines with other styles. Many of the techniques can be inserted into the transitions between postures in a form. This was something that was shared with me in my Yang Taiji training, where my teacher would at times insert Butterfly techniques. Later on, in 2013, I put together a complete Butterfly/Yang Fusion Set based upon our Yang Style short form, and performed it at a well-known national tournament. I received pre-penalty scores

Here is a diagram outlining the Shaolin Butterfly Style. As the diagram indicates, all aspects are inter-connected:

of 10, 10, and 9.9 (I went over the time limit and finished 3rd). Needless to say it was well accepted.

Other Training Methods

I was also exposed to Butterfly Tui Shou ("push hands"). Tui Shou training is a bridge between solo technique practice and sparring which allows one to develop various skills and practice the techniques in a controlled way. This was very similar to Taiji tui shou, just making use of the Butterfly techniques.

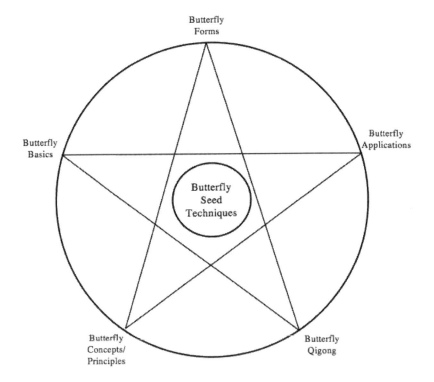

Butterfly Transformations

So, while the Shaolin Butterfly Style is an outstanding style in its own right, as the "inner connector style" of its Mother System—the Shaolin Five Form Fist System—it is invaluable. Training in this style leads to a doubling of speed and efficiency with all known techniques, and aids in being able to transform from one style and technique to another. There is no magic about this, either. These skills come from disciplined training and guidance from a properly trained Sifu.

One day after a seminar my teacher taught on this great, formerly "secret" style, he held out his open palm with fingers stretched apart to make a point. He started with his thumb and moved right to the pinkie finger, naming our main animal styles: Tiger (thumb), Leopard (index), Snake (middle), Crane (ring), Monkey (pinkie).

In the center of the palm he put the Butterfly and the Dragon. Both are styles of Transformation and Change. The Dragon aligned with Spirit/Heaven, and the Butterfly an Earthly symbol of change. Due to its importance, significance, and its beauty I like to think of the Shaolin Butterfly as the Heart of the Dragon. May our hearts be ever young and joyful, and all Dragons be blessed.

Aloha kakou, mahalonuiloa, a huihou.

Caption and Credit Page

1) L-R, Master Giancarlo Fusco, Sifu Dao Li Shen, myself, Sifu Donald Kinnie · xvi

2) The Hartford Courant, 10/8/1972 · · · · · · · · · · · · · · · · · 12

3) Dr. Daniel K. Pai, photo courtesy of Christopher Lee Helton · 13

4) Dr. Daniel K. Pai, Dragon Wing Ice Break, from CT Magazine, 1973, photo by Mr. David J. Everett · · · · · · 14

5) United States Karate Association Chief Instructor, Dr. Daniel K. Pai, standing 2nd from right; USKA Founder, GM Robert Trias, kneeling in center; USKA Chief Instructor, Dr. Maung Gyi, kneeling 2nd from right; Bill "Superfoot" Wallace, standing far left; GM Jim Cravens, standing 3rd from right; various other Masters and champions of the USKA · · · · · 15

6) Dr. Daniel K. Pai blindfolded and slicing a watermelon to pieces on the abdomen of his student, Yogi Israel Segarra, Hartford Courant early 1970's · · · · · 15

7) My teacher, Lao Shr Tao Chi Li, double butterfly knives, 1980 ·17

8) My teacher, Lao Shr Tao Chi Li, 1986 · · · · · · · · · · · · · · · 18

9) Sifu Michael Fuchs, brand new Assistant Instructor/ Shr Shyung, 1990 · 19

10) Dr. Daniel K. Pai, Bruce Lee, Grandmaster Jhoon Rhee, Grandmaster George Dillman, L-R, early 1960's, courtesy of Mr. George Dillman · · · · · · · · · · · · · · · · · · · 21

11) Sifu Michael Fuchs with Dr. Maung Gyi, circa 2004 · · · · · 22

12) Program of Koushu Demonstrations, White Dragon
    Society (Dr. Pai and Team), Taipei, Taiwan, 1976 · · · · · · 25
13) Dr. Daniel K. Pai being carried by the
    Taiwan Koushu Team at the 3rd World Koushu
    Games hosted by Dr. Pai in Hawaii, photo
    courtesy of GM Marcia Pickands · · · · · · · · · · · · · · · · · 26
14) Sifu Michael Fuchs, Wu Chun Taiji · · · · · · · · · · · · · · · · 29
15) Sifu Michael Fuchs, Dragon Wings · · · · · · · · · · · · · · · · 30
16) Sifu Michael Fuchs with Nine-Section Steel Whip · · · · · · 32
17) Dr. Daniel K. Pai, SGM Edmund Parker, GM
    George Dillman, getting ready to pick up
    Bruce Lee at the airport, early 1960's, photo
    courtesy of Mr. George Dillmanp · · · · · · · · · · · · · · · · · 62
18) "Four Winds Staff Seminar," led
    by Dr. Maung Gyi, 2003 ·142
19) Sifu Dao Li Shen, don dau (saber) · · · · · · · · · · · · · · · ·143

Author's Biography

Michael Fuchs is a lifelong reader and writer, enjoying many genres of literature, fiction, and non-fiction, as well as movies and television. A child of amazing artists, he was raised in an artistic environment which encouraged his creativity from birth. He has had editorials and articles published in magazines, such as *Massage Magazine, Tai Chi, Qi: The Journal of Eastern Health and Fitness*, and *The Empty Vessel*. He has been featured on television, radio, and in newspapers and magazines numerous times.

Mike is a Sifu (Master Teacher) and Instructor in the arts of Shaolin Five Form Fist Kung Fu, Taiji, Kali, Reiki, Qi Gong, Min Zin and Meditation. He is the former owner and Chief Instructor of the White Lotus Martial Arts Center (est. 1977) and currently leads Butterfly Martial and Healing Arts. He has been elected by his peers in the arts into elite Halls of Fame, including the Action Martial Arts Hall of Honors, The Master's Hall of Fame, and the World Karate Union 'Lifetime Achievement Award," amongst others.

Sifu Mike has been blessed to learn Reiki Healing Arts and related methods of Min Zin, Qi Gong, and Meditation from some of the most elite and renowned teachers of these arts. He has also received shaktipata, darshan, satsang, inititian and meditation instruction from famous world level spiritual leaders, such as: Sant Rajinder Singh ji Maharaj, Shri Anandi Ma, Mirabai Devi, Gen Sherab Kelsang, Namadeva Thomas Ashley-Farrand, and Self Realization Fellowship.

Reiki, Taiji, and Martial Arts teachers include famous living legend Dr. Maung Gyi, Susane Grasso and Pat Warren (2 of the pioneering reiki teachers in the Northeast, USA), Living Treasure Fu Shu Yun, 5 Form Fist Shaolin Headmaster Tao Chi LI, Tuhon Leo T. Gaje, Daoist Lineage Holder Prof. Chung Jie, Sifu Manfred Steiner, Master Wang Hai Jun, Sifu H.K. Chan, Tuhon Bill McGrath, and various others.

Sifu Mike has led Reiki Healing Art programs in the CT State Prison System and taught Reiki Certification Classes in the CT State Community College System for about 10 years. He was also part of the first class of professionally credentialed Integrative Medicine Consultants in the state of Connecticut, via St. Francis Hospital and Medical System (late 90's), and has led and taught numerous taiji, martial arts, and reiki healing arts multi-day retreats, workshops, seminars and other special events. Sifu Mike has had success integrating his arts of Reiki, Taiji, Qi Gong, Meditation and Min Zin with traditional medical/healthcare for many special needs groups for close to 30 years now. This includes the Arthritis Foundation, MS Society, Seniors, Prison Populations, Acute Care Rehabilitation and Psych. Settings, inner city youth, Spiritual and Religious Retreat settings, in the hospital and medical system/setting, and others. Recently he has led programs on Reiki and Taiji for the CT Brain Injury Alliance and Project Genesis, and is a Certified Brain Injury Specialist.

Sifu Mike has had success in the martial arts tournament scene as well, both as a trainer and competitor. He trained an extreme full contact weapons fighter who competed in The Gathering of the Pack (Dog Brothers). This young man went undefeated and credited Sifu Mike's training for his success. Later in life, Sifu Mike also attended multiple national and world martial art tourneys and had excellent success, such as receiving scores of 10, 10, and 9.9 for his performance of Butterfly/Yang style taiji at the well known Ocean State Grand Nationals in 2013. (He was penalized for going over the time limit and finished 3rd), amongst other similar results at national and world tourneys.

56865649R00146

Made in the USA
Middletown, DE
27 July 2019